Prince C
a Roma

Robert Louis Stevenson

Alpha Editions

This edition published in 2024

ISBN 9789362097385

Design and Setting By

Alpha Editions

www.alphaedis.com

Email - info@alphaedis.com

Contents

TO NELLY VAN DE GRIFT
(MRS. ADULFO SANCHEZ, OF MONTEREY)

At last, after so many years, I have the pleasure of re-introducing you to 'Prince Otto,' whom you will remember a very little fellow, no bigger in fact than a few sheets of memoranda written for me by your kind hand. The sight of his name will carry you back to an old wooden house embowered in creepers; a house that was far gone in the respectable stages of antiquity and seemed indissoluble from the green garden in which it stood, and that yet was a sea-traveller in its younger days, and had come round the Horn piecemeal in the belly of a ship, and might have heard the seamen stamping and shouting and the note of the boatswain's whistle. It will recall to you the nondescript inhabitants now so widely scattered:—the two horses, the dog, and the four cats, some of them still looking in your face as you read these lines;—the poor lady, so unfortunately married to an author;—the China boy, by this time, perhaps, baiting his line by the banks of a river in the Flowery Land;—and in particular the Scot who was then sick apparently unto death, and whom you did so much to cheer and keep in good behaviour.

You may remember that he was full of ambitions and designs: so soon as he had his health again completely, you may remember the fortune he was to earn, the journeys he was to go upon, the delights he was to enjoy and confer, and (among other matters) the masterpiece he was to make of 'Prince Otto'!

Well, we will not give in that we are finally beaten. We read together in those days the story of Braddock, and how, as he was carried dying from the scene of his defeat, he promised himself to do better another time: a story that will always touch a brave heart, and a dying speech worthy of a more fortunate commander. I try to be of Braddock's mind. I still mean to get my health again; I still purpose, by hook or crook, this book or the next, to launch a masterpiece; and I still intend—somehow, some time or other—to see your face and to hold your hand.

Meanwhile, this little paper traveller goes forth instead, crosses the great seas and the long plains and the dark mountains, and comes at last to your door in Monterey, charged with tender greetings. Pray you, take him in. He comes from a house where (even as in your own) there are gathered together some of the waifs of our company at Oakland: a house—for all its outlandish Gaelic name and distant station—where you are well-beloved.

R. L. S.

Skerryvore,
    Bournemouth.

BOOK I
PRINCE ERRANT

CHAPTER I
IN WHICH THE PRINCE DEPARTS ON AN ADVENTURE

You shall seek in vain upon the map of Europe for the bygone state of Grünewald. An independent principality, an infinitesimal member of the German Empire, she played, for several centuries, her part in the discord of Europe; and, at last, in the ripeness of time and at the spiriting of several bald diplomatists, vanished like a morning ghost. Less fortunate than Poland, she left not a regret behind her; and the very memory of her boundaries has faded.

It was a patch of hilly country covered with thick wood. Many streams took their beginning in the glens of Grünewald, turning mills for the inhabitants. There was one town, Mittwalden, and many brown, wooden hamlets, climbing roof above roof, along the steep bottom of dells, and communicating by covered bridges over the larger of the torrents. The hum of watermills, the splash of running water, the clean odour of pine sawdust, the sound and smell of the pleasant wind among the innumerable army of the mountain pines, the dropping fire of huntsmen, the dull stroke of the wood-axe, intolerable roads, fresh trout for supper in the clean bare chamber of an inn, and the song of birds and the music of the village-bells—these were the recollections of the Grünewald tourist.

North and east the foothills of Grünewald sank with varying profile into a vast plain. On these sides many small states bordered with the principality, Gerolstein, an extinct grand duchy, among the number. On the south it marched with the comparatively powerful kingdom of Seaboard Bohemia, celebrated for its flowers and mountain bears, and inhabited by a people of singular simplicity and tenderness of heart. Several intermarriages had, in the course of centuries, united the crowned families of Grünewald and Maritime Bohemia; and the last Prince of Grünewald, whose history I purpose to relate, drew his descent through Perdita, the only daughter of King Florizel the First of Bohemia. That these intermarriages had in some degree mitigated the rough, manly stock of the first Grünewalds, was an opinion widely held within the borders of the principality. The charcoal burner, the mountain sawyer, the wielder of the broad axe among the congregated pines of Grünewald, proud of their hard hands, proud of their shrewd ignorance and almost savage lore, looked with an unfeigned contempt on the soft character and manners of the sovereign race.

The precise year of grace in which this tale begins shall be left to the conjecture of the reader. But for the season of the year (which, in such a story, is the more important of the two) it was already so far forward in the spring, that when mountain people heard horns echoing all day about the north-west corner of the principality, they told themselves that Prince Otto and his hunt were up and out for the last time till the return of autumn.

At this point the borders of Grünewald descend somewhat steeply, here and there breaking into crags; and this shaggy and trackless country stands in a bold contrast to the cultivated plain below. It was traversed at that period by two roads alone; one, the imperial highway, bound to Brandenau in Gerolstein, descended the slope obliquely and by the easiest gradients. The other ran like a fillet across the very forehead of the hills, dipping into savage gorges, and wetted by the spray of tiny waterfalls. Once it passed beside a certain tower or castle, built sheer upon the margin of a formidable cliff, and commanding a vast prospect of the skirts of Grünewald and the busy plains of Gerolstein. The Felsenburg (so this tower was called) served now as a prison, now as a hunting-seat; and for all it stood so lonesome to the naked eye, with the aid of a good glass the burghers of Brandenau could count its windows from the lime-tree terrace where they walked at night.

In the wedge of forest hillside enclosed between the roads, the horns continued all day long to scatter tumult; and at length, as the sun began to draw near to the horizon of the plain, a rousing triumph announced the slaughter of the quarry. The first and second huntsman had drawn somewhat aside, and from the summit of a knoll gazed down before them on the drooping shoulders of the hill and across the expanse of plain. They covered their eyes, for the sun was in their faces. The glory of its going down was somewhat pale. Through the confused tracery of many thousands of naked poplars, the smoke of so many houses, and the evening steam ascending from the fields, the sails of a windmill on a gentle eminence moved very conspicuously, like a donkey's ears. And hard by, like an open gash, the imperial high-road ran straight sun-ward, an artery of travel.

There is one of nature's spiritual ditties, that has not yet been set to words or human music: 'The Invitation to the Road'; an air continually sounding in the ears of gipsies, and to whose inspiration our nomadic fathers journeyed all their days. The hour, the season, and the scene, all were in delicate accordance. The air was full of birds of passage, steering westward and northward over Grünewald, an army of specks to the up-looking eye. And below, the great practicable road was bound for the same quarter.

But to the two horsemen on the knoll this spiritual ditty was unheard. They were, indeed, in some concern of mind, scanning every fold of the subjacent forest, and betraying both anger and dismay in their impatient gestures.

'I do not see him, Kuno,' said the first huntsman, 'nowhere—not a trace, not a hair of the mare's tail! No, sir, he's off; broke cover and got away. Why, for twopence I would hunt him with the dogs!'

'Mayhap, he's gone home,' said Kuno, but without conviction.

'Home!' sneered the other. 'I give him twelve days to get home. No, it's begun again; it's as it was three years ago, before he married; a disgrace! Hereditary prince, hereditary fool! There goes the government over the borders on a grey mare. What's that? No, nothing—no, I tell you, on my word, I set more store by a good gelding or an English dog. That for your Otto!'

'He's not my Otto,' growled Kuno.

'Then I don't know whose he is,' was the retort.

'You would put your hand in the fire for him to-morrow,' said Kuno, facing round.

'Me!' cried the huntsman. 'I would see him hanged! I'm a Grünewald patriot—enrolled, and have my medal, too; and I would help a prince! I'm for liberty and Gondremark.'

'Well, it's all one,' said Kuno. 'If anybody said what you said, you would have his blood, and you know it.'

'You have him on the brain,' retorted his companion. 'There he goes!' he cried, the next moment.

And sure enough, about a mile down the mountain, a rider on a white horse was seen to flit rapidly across a heathy open and vanish among the trees on the farther side.

'In ten minutes he'll be over the border into Gerolstein,' said Kuno. 'It's past cure.'

'Well, if he founders that mare, I'll never forgive him,' added the other, gathering his reins.

And as they turned down from the knoll to rejoin their comrades, the sun dipped and disappeared, and the woods fell instantly into the gravity and greyness of the early night.

CHAPTER II
IN WHICH THE PRINCE PLAYS
HAROUN-AL-RASCHID

The night fell upon the Prince while he was threading green tracks in the lower valleys of the wood; and though the stars came out overhead and displayed the interminable order of the pine-tree pyramids, regular and dark like cypresses, their light was of small service to a traveller in such lonely paths, and from thenceforth he rode at random. The austere face of nature, the uncertain issue of his course, the open sky and the free air, delighted him like wine; and the hoarse chafing of a river on his left sounded in his ears agreeably.

It was past eight at night before his toil was rewarded and he issued at last out of the forest on the firm white high-road. It lay downhill before him, with a sweeping eastward trend, faintly bright between the thickets; and Otto paused and gazed upon it. So it ran, league after league, still joining others, to the farthest ends of Europe, there skirting the sea-surge, here gleaming in the lights of cities; and the innumerable army of tramps and travellers moved upon it in all lands as by a common impulse, and were now in all places drawing near to the inn door and the night's rest. The pictures swarmed and vanished in his brain; a surge of temptation, a beat of all his blood, went over him, to set spur to the mare and to go into the unknown for ever. And then it passed away; hunger and fatigue, and that habit of middling actions which we call common sense, resumed their empire; and in that changed mood his eye lighted upon two bright windows on his left hand, between the road and river.

He turned off by a by-road, and in a few minutes he was knocking with his whip on the door of a large farmhouse, and a chorus of dogs from the farmyard were making angry answer. A very tall, old, white-headed man came, shading a candle, at the summons. He had been of great strength in his time, and of a handsome countenance; but now he was fallen away, his teeth were quite gone, and his voice when he spoke was broken and falsetto.

'You will pardon me,' said Otto. 'I am a traveller and have entirely lost my way.'

'Sir,' said the old man, in a very stately, shaky manner, 'you are at the River Farm, and I am Killian Gottesheim, at your disposal. We are here, sir, at about an equal distance from Mittwalden in Grünewald and Brandenau in

Gerolstein: six leagues to either, and the road excellent; but there is not a wine bush, not a carter's alehouse, anywhere between. You will have to accept my hospitality for the night; rough hospitality, to which I make you freely welcome; for, sir,' he added with a bow, 'it is God who sends the guest.'

'Amen. And I most heartily thank you,' replied Otto, bowing in his turn.

'Fritz,' said the old man, turning towards the interior, 'lead round this gentleman's horse; and you, sir, condescend to enter.'

Otto entered a chamber occupying the greater part of the ground-floor of the building. It had probably once been divided; for the farther end was raised by a long step above the nearer, and the blazing fire and the white supper-table seemed to stand upon a daïs. All around were dark, brass-mounted cabinets and cupboards; dark shelves carrying ancient country crockery; guns and antlers and broadside ballads on the wall; a tall old clock with roses on the dial; and down in one corner the comfortable promise of a wine barrel. It was homely, elegant, and quaint.

A powerful youth hurried out to attend on the grey mare; and when Mr. Killian Gottesheim had presented him to his daughter Ottilia, Otto followed to the stable as became, not perhaps the Prince, but the good horseman. When he returned, a smoking omelette and some slices of home-cured ham were waiting him; these were followed by a ragout and a cheese; and it was not until his guest had entirely satisfied his hunger, and the whole party drew about the fire over the wine jug, that Killian Gottesheim's elaborate courtesy permitted him to address a question to the Prince.

'You have perhaps ridden far, sir?' he inquired.

'I have, as you say, ridden far,' replied Otto; 'and, as you have seen, I was prepared to do justice to your daughters cookery.'

'Possibly, sir, from the direction of Brandenau?' continued Killian.

'Precisely: and I should have slept to-night, had I not wandered, in Mittwalden,' answered the Prince, weaving in a patch of truth, according to the habit of all liars.

'Business leads you to Mittwalden?' was the next question.

'Mere curiosity,' said Otto. 'I have never yet visited the principality of Grünewald.'

'A pleasant state, sir,' piped the old man, nodding, 'a very pleasant state, and a fine race, both pines and people. We reckon ourselves part Grünewalders here, lying so near the borders; and the river there is all good

Grünewald water, every drop of it. Yes, sir, a fine state. A man of Grünewald now will swing me an axe over his head that many a man of Gerolstein could hardly lift; and the pines, why, deary me, there must be more pines in that little state, sir, than people in this whole big world. 'Tis twenty years now since I crossed the marshes, for we grow home-keepers in old age; but I mind it as if it was yesterday. Up and down, the road keeps right on from here to Mittwalden; and nothing all the way but the good green pine-trees, big and little, and water-power! water-power at every step, sir. We once sold a bit of forest, up there beside the high-road; and the sight of minted money that we got for it has set me ciphering ever since what all the pines in Grünewald would amount to.'

'I suppose you see nothing of the Prince?' inquired Otto.

'No,' said the young man, speaking for the first time, 'nor want to.'

'Why so? is he so much disliked?' asked Otto.

'Not what you might call disliked,' replied the old gentleman, 'but despised, sir.'

'Indeed,' said the Prince, somewhat faintly.

'Yes, sir, despised,' nodded Killian, filling a long pipe, 'and, to my way of thinking, justly despised. Here is a man with great opportunities, and what does he do with them? He hunts, and he dresses very prettily—which is a thing to be ashamed of in a man—and he acts plays; and if he does aught else, the news of it has not come here.'

'Yet these are all innocent,' said Otto. 'What would you have him do—make war?'

'No, sir,' replied the old man. 'But here it is; I have been fifty years upon this River Farm, and wrought in it, day in, day out; I have ploughed and sowed and reaped, and risen early, and waked late; and this is the upshot: that all these years it has supported me and my family; and been the best friend that ever I had, set aside my wife; and now, when my time comes, I leave it a better farm than when I found it. So it is, if a man works hearty in the order of nature, he gets bread and he receives comfort, and whatever he touches breeds. And it humbly appears to me, if that Prince was to labour on his throne, as I have laboured and wrought in my farm, he would find both an increase and a blessing.'

'I believe with you, sir,' Otto said; 'and yet the parallel is inexact. For the farmer's life is natural and simple; but the prince's is both artificial and complicated. It is easy to do right in the one, and exceedingly difficult not to do wrong in the other. If your crop is blighted, you can take off your bonnet and say, "God's will be done"; but if the prince meets with a reverse, he may have to blame himself for the attempt. And perhaps, if all the kings in Europe were to confine themselves to innocent amusement, the subjects would be the better off.'

'Ay,' said the young man Fritz, 'you are in the right of it there. That was a true word spoken. And I see you are like me, a good patriot and an enemy to princes.'

Otto was somewhat abashed at this deduction, and he made haste to change his ground. 'But,' said he, 'you surprise me by what you say of this Prince Otto. I have heard him, I must own, more favourably painted. I was told he was, in his heart, a good fellow, and the enemy of no one but himself.'

'And so he is, sir,' said the girl, 'a very handsome, pleasant prince; and we know some who would shed their blood for him.'

'O! Kuno!' said Fritz. 'An ignoramus!'

'Ay, Kuno, to be sure,' quavered the old farmer. 'Well, since this gentleman is a stranger to these parts, and curious about the Prince, I do believe that story might divert him. This Kuno, you must know, sir, is one of the hunt servants, and a most ignorant, intemperate man: a right Grünewalder, as we say in Gerolstein. We know him well, in this house; for he has come as far as here after his stray dogs; and I make all welcome, sir, without account of state or nation. And, indeed, between Gerolstein and Grünewald the peace has held so long that the roads stand open like my door; and a man will make no more of the frontier than the very birds themselves.'

'Ay,' said Otto, 'it has been a long peace—a peace of centuries.'

'Centuries, as you say,' returned Killian; 'the more the pity that it should not be for ever. Well, sir, this Kuno was one day in fault, and Otto, who has a quick temper, up with his whip and thrashed him, they do say, soundly. Kuno took it as best he could, but at last he broke out, and dared the Prince to throw his whip away and wrestle like a man; for we are all great at wrestling in these parts, and it's so that we generally settle our disputes. Well, sir, the Prince did so; and, being a weakly creature, found the tables turned; for the man whom he had just been thrashing like a negro slave, lifted him with a back grip and threw him heels overhead.'

'He broke his bridle-arm,' cried Fritz—'and some say his nose. Serve him right, say I! Man to man, which is the better at that?'

'And then?' asked Otto.

'O, then Kuno carried him home; and they were the best of friends from that day forth. I don't say it's a discreditable story, you observe,' continued

Mr. Gottesheim; 'but it's droll, and that's the fact. A man should think before he strikes; for, as my nephew says, man to man was the old valuation.'

'Now, if you were to ask me,' said Otto, 'I should perhaps surprise you. I think it was the Prince that conquered.'

'And, sir, you would be right,' replied Killian seriously. 'In the eyes of God, I do not question but you would be right; but men, sir, look at these things differently, and they laugh.'

'They made a song of it,' observed Fritz. 'How does it go? Ta-tum-ta-ra . . ?'

'Well,' interrupted Otto, who had no great anxiety to hear the song, 'the Prince is young; he may yet mend.'

'Not so young, by your leave,' cried Fritz. 'A man of forty.'

'Thirty-six,' corrected Mr. Gottesheim.

'O,' cried Ottilia, in obvious disillusion, 'a man of middle age! And they said he was so handsome when he was young!'

'And bald, too,' added Fritz.

Otto passed his hand among his locks. At that moment he was far from happy, and even the tedious evenings at Mittwalden Palace began to smile upon him by comparison.

'O, six-and-thirty!' he protested. 'A man is not yet old at six-and-thirty. I am that age myself.'

'I should have taken you for more, sir,' piped the old farmer. 'But if that be so, you are of an age with Master Ottekin, as people call him; and, I would wager a crown, have done more service in your time. Though it seems young by comparison with men of a great age like me, yet it's some way through life for all that; and the mere fools and fiddlers are beginning to grow weary and to look old. Yes, sir, by six-and-thirty, if a man be a follower of God's laws, he should have made himself a home and a good name to live by; he should have got a wife and a blessing on his marriage; and his works, as the Word says, should begin to follow him.'

'Ah, well, the Prince is married,' cried Fritz, with a coarse burst of laughter.

'That seems to entertain you, sir,' said Otto.

'Ay,' said the young boor. 'Did you not know that? I thought all Europe knew it!' And he added a pantomime of a nature to explain his accusation to the dullest.

'Ah, sir,' said Mr. Gottesheim, 'it is very plain that you are not from hereabouts! But the truth is, that the whole princely family and Court are rips and rascals, not one to mend another. They live, sir, in idleness and—what most commonly follows it—corruption. The Princess has a lover—a Baron, as he calls himself, from East Prussia; and the Prince is so little of a man, sir, that he holds the candle. Nor is that the worst of it, for this foreigner and his paramour are suffered to transact the State affairs, while the Prince takes the salary and leaves all things to go to wrack. There will follow upon this some manifest judgment which, though I am old, I may survive to see.'

'Good man, you are in the wrong about Gondremark,' said Fritz, showing a greatly increased animation; 'but for all the rest, you speak the God's truth like a good patriot. As for the Prince, if he would take and strangle his wife, I would forgive him yet.'

'Nay, Fritz,' said the old man, 'that would be to add iniquity to evil. For you perceive, sir,' he continued, once more addressing himself to the unfortunate Prince, 'this Otto has himself to thank for these disorders. He has his young wife and his principality, and he has sworn to cherish both.'

'Sworn at the altar!' echoed Fritz. 'But put your faith in princes!'

'Well, sir, he leaves them both to an adventurer from East Prussia,' pursued the farmer: 'leaves the girl to be seduced and to go on from bad to worse, till her name's become a tap-room by-word, and she not yet twenty; leaves the country to be overtaxed, and bullied with armaments, and jockied into war—'

'War!' cried Otto.

'So they say, sir; those that watch their ongoings, say to war,' asseverated Killian. 'Well, sir, that is very sad; it is a sad thing for this poor, wicked girl to go down to hell with people's curses; it's a sad thing for a tight little happy country to be misconducted; but whoever may complain, I humbly conceive, sir, that this Otto cannot. What he has worked for, that he has got; and may God have pity on his soul, for a great and a silly sinner's!'

'He has broke his oath; then he is a perjurer. He takes the money and leaves the work; why, then plainly he's a thief. A cuckold he was before, and a fool by birth. Better me that!' cried Fritz, and snapped his fingers.

'And now, sir, you will see a little,' continued the farmer, 'why we think so poorly of this Prince Otto. There's such a thing as a man being pious and honest in the private way; and there is such a thing, sir, as a public virtue; but when a man has neither, the Lord lighten him! Even this Gondremark, that Fritz here thinks so much of—'

'Ay,' interrupted Fritz, 'Gondremark's the man for me. I would we had his like in Gerolstein.'

'He is a bad man,' said the old farmer, shaking his head; 'and there was never good begun by the breach of God's commandments. But so far I will go with you; he is a man that works for what he has.'

'I tell you he's the hope of Grünewald,' cried Fritz. 'He doesn't suit some of your high-and-dry, old, ancient ideas; but he's a downright modern man—a man of the new lights and the progress of the age. He does some things wrong; so they all do; but he has the people's interests next his heart; and you mark me—you, sir, who are a Liberal, and the enemy of all their governments, you please to mark my words—the day will come in Grünewald, when they take out that yellow-headed skulk of a Prince and that dough-faced Messalina of a Princess, march 'em back foremost over the borders, and proclaim the Baron Gondremark first President. I've heard them say it in a speech. I was at a meeting once at Brandenau, and the Mittwalden delegates spoke up for fifteen thousand. Fifteen thousand, all brigaded, and each man with a medal round his neck to rally by. That's all Gondremark.'

'Ay, sir, you see what it leads to; wild talk to-day, and wilder doings to-morrow,' said the old man. 'For there is one thing certain: that this Gondremark has one foot in the Court backstairs, and the other in the Masons' lodges. He gives himself out, sir, for what nowadays they call a patriot: a man from East Prussia!'

'Give himself out!' cried Fritz. 'He is! He is to lay by his title as soon as the Republic is declared; I heard it in a speech.'

'Lay by Baron to take up President?' returned Killian. 'King Log, King Stork. But you'll live longer than I, and you will see the fruits of it.'

'Father,' whispered Ottilia, pulling at the speaker's coat, 'surely the gentleman is ill.'

'I beg your pardon,' cried the farmer, rewaking to hospitable thoughts; 'can I offer you anything?'

'I thank you. I am very weary,' answered Otto. 'I have presumed upon my strength. If you would show me to a bed, I should be grateful.'

'Ottilia, a candle!' said the old man. 'Indeed, sir, you look paley. A little cordial water? No? Then follow me, I beseech you, and I will bring you to the stranger's bed. You are not the first by many who has slept well below my roof,' continued the old gentleman, mounting the stairs before his guest; 'for good food, honest wine, a grateful conscience, and a little pleasant chat before a man retires, are worth all the possets and apothecary's drugs. See, sir,' and here he opened a door and ushered Otto into a little white-washed sleeping-room, 'here you are in port. It is small, but it is airy, and the sheets are clean and kept in lavender. The window, too, looks out above the river, and there's no music like a little river's. It plays the same tune (and that's the favourite) over and over again, and yet does not weary of it like men fiddlers. It takes the mind out of doors: and though we should be grateful for good houses, there is, after all, no house like God's out-of-doors. And lastly, sir, it quiets a man down like saying his prayers. So here, sir, I take my kind leave of you until to-morrow; and it is my prayerful wish that you may slumber like a prince.'

And the old man, with the twentieth courteous inclination, left his guest alone.

CHAPTER III
IN WHICH THE PRINCE COMFORTS AGE
AND BEAUTY AND DELIVERS A LECTURE
ON DISCRETION IN LOVE

The Prince was early abroad: in the time of the first chorus of birds, of the pure and quiet air, of the slanting sunlight and the mile-long shadows. To one who had passed a miserable night, the freshness of that hour was tonic and reviving; to steal a march upon his slumbering fellows, to be the Adam of the coming day, composed and fortified his spirits; and the Prince, breathing deep and pausing as he went, walked in the wet fields beside his shadow, and was glad.

A trellised path led down into the valley of the brook, and he turned to follow it. The stream was a break-neck, boiling Highland river. Hard by the farm, it leaped a little precipice in a thick grey-mare's tail of twisted filaments, and then lay and worked and bubbled in a lynn. Into the middle of this quaking pool a rock protruded, shelving to a cape; and thither Otto scrambled and sat down to ponder.

Soon the sun struck through the screen of branches and thin early leaves that made a hanging bower above the fall; and the golden lights and flitting shadows fell upon and marbled the surface of that so seething pot; and rays plunged deep among the turning waters; and a spark, as bright as a diamond, lit upon the swaying eddy. It began to grow warm where Otto lingered, warm and heady; the lights swam, weaving their maze across the shaken pool; on the impending rock, reflections danced like butterflies; and the air was fanned by the waterfall as by a swinging curtain.

Otto, who was weary with tossing and beset with horrid phantoms of remorse and jealousy, instantly fell dead in love with that sun-chequered, echoing corner. Holding his feet, he stared out of a drowsy trance, wondering, admiring, musing, losing his way among uncertain thoughts. There is nothing that so apes the external bearing of free will as that unconscious bustle, obscurely following liquid laws, with which a river contends among obstructions. It seems the very play of man and destiny, and as Otto pored on these recurrent changes, he grew, by equal steps, the sleepier and the more profound. Eddy and Prince were alike jostled in their purpose, alike anchored by intangible influences in one corner of the world. Eddy and Prince were alike useless, starkly useless, in the cosmology of men. Eddy and Prince—Prince and Eddy.

It is probable he had been some while asleep when a voice recalled him from oblivion. 'Sir,' it was saying; and looking round, he saw Mr. Killian's daughter, terrified by her boldness and making bashful signals from the shore. She was a plain, honest lass, healthy and happy and good, and with that sort of beauty that comes of happiness and health. But her confusion lent her for the moment an additional charm.

'Good-morning,' said Otto, rising and moving towards her. 'I arose early and was in a dream.'

'O, sir!' she cried, 'I wish to beg of you to spare my father; for I assure your Highness, if he had known who you was, he would have bitten his tongue out sooner. And Fritz, too—how he went on! But I had a notion; and this morning I went straight down into the stable, and there was your Highness's crown upon the stirrup-irons! But, O, sir, I made certain you would spare them; for they were as innocent as lambs.'

'My dear,' said Otto, both amused and gratified, 'you do not understand. It is I who am in the wrong; for I had no business to conceal my name and lead on these gentleman to speak of me. And it is I who have to beg of you that you will keep my secret and not betray the discourtesy of which I was guilty. As for any fear of me, your friends are safe in Gerolstein; and even in my own territory, you must be well aware I have no power.'

'O, sir,' she said, curtsying, 'I would not say that: the huntsmen would all die for you.'

'Happy Prince!' said Otto. 'But although you are too courteous to avow the knowledge, you have had many opportunities of learning that I am a vain show. Only last night we heard it very clearly stated. You see the shadow flitting on this hard rock? Prince Otto, I am afraid, is but the moving shadow, and the name of the rock is Gondremark. Ah! if your friends had fallen foul of Gondremark! But happily the younger of the two admires him. And as for the old gentleman your father, he is a wise man and an excellent talker, and I would take a long wager he is honest.'

'O, for honest, your Highness, that he is!' exclaimed the girl. 'And Fritz is as honest as he. And as for all they said, it was just talk and nonsense. When countryfolk get gossiping, they go on, I do assure you, for the fun; they don't as much as think of what they say. If you went to the next farm, it's my belief you would hear as much against my father.'

'Nay, nay,' said Otto, 'there you go too fast. For all that was said against Prince Otto—'

'O, it was shameful!' cried the girl.

'Not shameful—true,' returned Otto. 'O, yes—true. I am all they said of me—all that and worse.'

'I never!' cried 'Ottilia. 'Is that how you do? Well, you would never be a soldier. Now if any one accuses me, I get up and give it them. O, I defend myself. I wouldn't take a fault at another person's hands, no, not if I had it on my forehead. And that's what you must do, if you mean to live it out. But, indeed, I never heard such nonsense. I should think you was ashamed of yourself! You're bald, then, I suppose?'

'O no,' said Otto, fairly laughing. 'There I acquit myself: not bald!'

'Well, and good?' pursued the girl. 'Come now, you know you are good, and I'll make you say so . . . Your Highness, I beg your humble pardon. But there's no disrespect intended. And anyhow, you know you are.'

'Why, now, what am I to say?' replied Otto. 'You are a cook, and excellently well you do it; I embrace the chance of thanking you for the ragout. Well now, have you not seen good food so bedevilled by unskilful cookery that no one could be brought to eat the pudding? That is me, my dear. I am full of good ingredients, but the dish is worthless. I am—I give it you in one word—sugar in the salad.'

'Well, I don't care, you're good,' reiterated Ottilia, a little flushed by having failed to understand.

'I will tell you one thing,' replied Otto: 'You are!'

'Ah, well, that's what they all said of you,' moralised the girl; 'such a tongue to come round—such a flattering tongue!'

'O, you forget, I am a man of middle age,' the Prince chuckled.

'Well, to speak to you, I should think you was a boy; and Prince or no Prince, if you came worrying where I was cooking, I would pin a napkin to your tails. . . . And, O Lord, I declare I hope your Highness will forgive me,' the girl added. 'I can't keep it in my mind.'

'No more can I,' cried Otto. 'That is just what they complain of!'

They made a loverly-looking couple; only the heavy pouring of that horse-tail of water made them raise their voices above lovers' pitch. But to a jealous onlooker from above, their mirth and close proximity might easily give umbrage; and a rough voice out of a tuft of brambles began calling on Ottilia by name. She changed colour at that. 'It is Fritz,' she said. 'I must go.'

'Go, my dear, and I need not bid you go in peace, for I think you have discovered that I am not formidable at close quarters,' said the Prince, and made her a fine gesture of dismissal.

So Ottilia skipped up the bank, and disappeared into the thicket, stopping once for a single blushing bob—blushing, because she had in the interval once more forgotten and remembered the stranger's quality.

Otto returned to his rock promontory; but his humour had in the meantime changed. The sun now shone more fairly on the pool; and over its brown, welling surface, the blue of heaven and the golden green of the spring foliage danced in fleeting arabesque. The eddies laughed and brightened with essential colour. And the beauty of the dell began to rankle in the Prince's mind; it was so near to his own borders, yet without. He had never had much of the joy of possessorship in any of the thousand and one beautiful and curious things that were his; and now he was conscious of envy for what was another's. It was, indeed, a smiling, dilettante sort of envy; but yet there it was: the passion of Ahab for the vineyard, done in little; and he was relieved when Mr. Killian appeared upon the scene.

'I hope, sir, that you have slept well under my plain roof,' said the old farmer.

'I am admiring this sweet spot that you are privileged to dwell in,' replied Otto, evading the inquiry.

'It is rustic,' returned Mr. Gottesheim, looking around him with complacency, 'a very rustic corner; and some of the land to the west is most excellent fat land, excellent deep soil. You should see my wheat in the ten-acre field. There is not a farm in Grünewald, no, nor many in Gerolstein, to match the River Farm. Some sixty—I keep thinking when I sow—some sixty, and some seventy, and some an hundredfold; and my own place, six score! But that, sir, is partly the farming.'

'And the stream has fish?' asked Otto.

'A fish-pond,' said the farmer. 'Ay, it is a pleasant bit. It is pleasant even here, if one had time, with the brook drumming in that black pool, and the green things hanging all about the rocks, and, dear heart, to see the very pebbles! all turned to gold and precious stones! But you have come to that time of life, sir, when, if you will excuse me, you must look to have the rheumatism set in. Thirty to forty is, as one may say, their seed-time. And this is a damp cold corner for the early morning and an empty stomach. If I might humbly advise you, sir, I would be moving.'

'With all my heart,' said Otto gravely. 'And so you have lived your life here?' he added, as they turned to go.

'Here I was born,' replied the farmer, 'and here I wish I could say I was to die. But fortune, sir, fortune turns the wheel. They say she is blind, but we will hope she only sees a little farther on. My grandfather and my father and I, we have all tilled these acres, my furrow following theirs. All the three names are on the garden bench, two Killians and one Johann. Yes, sir, good men have prepared themselves for the great change in my old garden. Well do I mind my father, in a woollen night-cap, the good soul, going round and round to see the last of it. 'Killian,' said he, 'do you see the smoke of my tobacco? Why,' said he, 'that is man's life.' It was his last pipe, and I believe he knew it; and it was a strange thing, without doubt, to leave the trees that he had planted, and the son that he had begotten, ay, sir, and even the old pipe with the Turk's head that he had smoked since he was a lad and went a-courting. But here we have no continuing city; and as for the eternal, it's a comfortable thought that we have other merits than our own. And yet you would hardly think how sore it goes against the grain with me, to die in a strange bed.'

'And must you do so? For what reason?' Otto asked.

'The reason? The place is to be sold; three thousand crowns,' replied Mr. Gottesheim. 'Had it been a third of that, I may say without boasting that, what with my credit and my savings, I could have met the sum. But at three thousand, unless I have singular good fortune and the new proprietor continues me in office, there is nothing left me but to budge.'

Otto's fancy for the place redoubled at the news, and became joined with other feelings. If all he heard were true, Grünewald was growing very hot for a sovereign Prince; it might be well to have a refuge; and if so, what more delightful hermitage could man imagine? Mr. Gottesheim, besides, had touched his sympathies. Every man loves in his soul to play the part of the stage deity. And to step down to the aid of the old farmer, who had so roughly handled him in talk, was the ideal of a Fair Revenge. Otto's thoughts brightened at the prospect, and he began to regard himself with a renewed respect.

'I can find you, I believe, a purchaser,' he said, 'and one who would continue to avail himself of your skill.'

'Can you, sir, indeed?' said the old man. 'Well, I shall be heartily obliged; for I begin to find a man may practise resignation all his days, as he takes physic, and not come to like it in the end.'

'If you will have the papers drawn, you may even burthen the purchase with your interest,' said Otto. 'Let it be assured to you through life.'

'Your friend, sir,' insinuated Killian, 'would not, perhaps, care to make the interest reversible? Fritz is a good lad.'

'Fritz is young,' said the Prince dryly; 'he must earn consideration, not inherit.'

'He has long worked upon the place, sir,' insisted Mr. Gottesheim; 'and at my great age, for I am seventy-eight come harvest, it would be a troublesome thought to the proprietor how to fill my shoes. It would be a care spared to assure yourself of Fritz. And I believe he might be tempted by a permanency.'

'The young man has unsettled views,' returned Otto.

'Possibly the purchaser—' began Killian.

A little spot of anger burned in Otto's cheek. 'I am the purchaser,' he said.

'It was what I might have guessed,' replied the farmer, bowing with an aged, obsequious dignity. 'You have made an old man very happy; and I may say, indeed, that I have entertained an angel unawares. Sir, the great people of this world—and by that I mean those who are great in station—if they had only hearts like yours, how they would make the fires burn and the poor sing!'

'I would not judge them hardly, sir,' said Otto. 'We all have our frailties.'

'Truly, sir,' said Mr. Gottesheim, with unction. 'And by what name, sir, am I to address my generous landlord?'

The double recollection of an English traveller, whom he had received the week before at court, and of an old English rogue called Transome, whom he had known in youth, came pertinently to the Prince's help. 'Transome,' he answered, 'is my name. I am an English traveller. It is, to-day, Tuesday. On Thursday, before noon, the money shall be ready. Let us meet, if you please, in Mittwalden, at the "Morning Star."'

'I am, in all things lawful, your servant to command,' replied the farmer. 'An Englishman! You are a great race of travellers. And has your lordship some experience of land?'

'I have had some interest of the kind before,' returned the Prince; 'not in Gerolstein, indeed. But fortune, as you say, turns the wheel, and I desire to be beforehand with her revolutions.'

'Very right, sir, I am sure,' said Mr. Killian.

They had been strolling with deliberation; but they were now drawing near to the farmhouse, mounting by the trellised pathway to the level of the meadow. A little before them, the sound of voices had been some while audible, and now grew louder and more distinct with every step of their advance. Presently, when they emerged upon the top of the bank, they beheld Fritz and Ottilia some way off; he, very black and bloodshot, emphasising his hoarse speech with the smacking of his fist against his palm; she, standing a little way off in blowsy, voluble distress.

'Dear me!' said Mr. Gottesheim, and made as if he would turn aside.

But Otto went straight towards the lovers, in whose dissension he believed himself to have a share. And, indeed, as soon as he had seen the Prince, Fritz had stood tragic, as if awaiting and defying his approach.

'O, here you are!' he cried, as soon as they were near enough for easy speech. 'You are a man at least, and must reply. What were you after? Why were you two skulking in the bush? God!' he broke out, turning again upon Ottilia, 'to think that I should waste my heart on you!'

'I beg your pardon,' Otto cut in. 'You were addressing me. In virtue of what circumstance am I to render you an account of this young lady's conduct? Are you her father? her brother? her husband?'

'O, sir, you know as well as I,' returned the peasant. 'We keep company, she and I. I love her, and she is by way of loving me; but all shall be above-board, I would have her to know. I have a good pride of my own.'

'Why, I perceive I must explain to you what love is,' said Otto. 'Its measure is kindness. It is very possible that you are proud; but she, too, may have some self-esteem; I do not speak for myself. And perhaps, if your own doings were so curiously examined, you might find it inconvenient to reply.'

'These are all set-offs,' said the young man. 'You know very well that a man is a man, and a woman only a woman. That holds good all over, up and down. I ask you a question, I ask it again, and here I stand.' He drew a mark and toed it.

'When you have studied liberal doctrines somewhat deeper,' said the Prince, 'you will perhaps change your note. You are a man of false weights and measures, my young friend. You have one scale for women, another for men; one for princes, and one for farmer-folk. On the prince who neglects his wife you can be most severe. But what of the lover who insults his mistress? You use the name of love. I should think this lady might very fairly ask to be delivered from love of such a nature. For if I, a stranger, had been one-tenth part so gross and so discourteous, you would most righteously have broke my head. It would have been in your part, as lover, to protect her from such insolence. Protect her first, then, from yourself.'

'Ay,' quoth Mr. Gottesheim, who had been looking on with his hands behind his tall old back, 'ay, that's Scripture truth.'

Fritz was staggered, not only by the Prince's imperturbable superiority of manner, but by a glimmering consciousness that he himself was in the wrong. The appeal to liberal doctrines had, besides, unmanned him.

'Well,' said he, 'if I was rude, I'll own to it. I meant no ill, and did nothing out of my just rights; but I am above all these old vulgar notions too; and if I spoke sharp, I'll ask her pardon.'

'Freely granted, Fritz,' said Ottilia.

'But all this doesn't answer me,' cried Fritz. 'I ask what you two spoke about. She says she promised not to tell; well, then, I mean to know. Civility is civility, but I'll be no man's gull. I have a right to common justice, if I *do* keep company!'

'If you will ask Mr. Gottesheim,' replied Otto, 'you will find I have not spent my hours in idleness. I have, since I arose this morning, agreed to buy the farm. So far I will go to satisfy a curiosity which I condemn.'

'O, well, if there was business, that's another matter,' returned Fritz. 'Though it beats me why you could not tell. But, of course, if the gentleman is to buy the farm, I suppose there would naturally be an end.'

'To be sure,' said Mr. Gottesheim, with a strong accent of conviction.

But Ottilia was much braver. 'There now!' she cried in triumph. 'What did I tell you? I told you I was fighting your battles. Now you see! Think shame of your suspicious temper! You should go down upon your bended knees both to that gentleman and me.'

CHAPTER IV
IN WHICH THE PRINCE COLLECTS
OPINIONS BY THE WAY

A little before noon Otto, by a triumph of manoeuvring, effected his escape. He was quit in this way of the ponderous gratitude of Mr. Killian, and of the confidential gratitude of poor Ottilia; but of Fritz he was not quit so readily. That young politician, brimming with mysterious glances, offered to lend his convoy as far as to the high-road; and Otto, in fear of some residuary jealousy and for the girl's sake, had not the courage to gainsay him; but he regarded his companion with uneasy glances, and devoutly wished the business at an end. For some time Fritz walked by the mare in silence; and they had already traversed more than half the proposed distance when, with something of a blush, he looked up and opened fire.

'Are you not,' he asked, 'what they call a socialist?'

'Why, no,' returned Otto, 'not precisely what they call so. Why do you ask?'

'I will tell you why,' said the young man. 'I saw from the first that you were a red progressional, and nothing but the fear of old Killian kept you back. And there, sir, you were right: old men are always cowards. But nowadays, you see, there are so many groups: you can never tell how far the likeliest kind of man may be prepared to go; and I was never sure you were one of the strong thinkers, till you hinted about women and free love.'

'Indeed,' cried Otto, 'I never said a word of such a thing.'

'Not you!' cried Fritz. 'Never a word to compromise! You was sowing seed: ground-bait, our president calls it. But it's hard to deceive me, for I know all the agitators and their ways, and all the doctrines; and between you and me,' lowering his voice, 'I am myself affiliated. O yes, I am a secret society man, and here is my medal.' And drawing out a green ribbon that he wore about his neck, he held up, for Otto's inspection, a pewter medal bearing the imprint of a Phoenix and the legend *Libertas*. 'And so now you see you may trust me,' added Fritz, 'I am none of your alehouse talkers; I am a convinced revolutionary.' And he looked meltingly upon Otto.

'I see,' replied the Prince; 'that is very gratifying. Well, sir, the great thing for the good of one's country is, first of all, to be a good man. All springs from there. For my part, although you are right in thinking that I have to do with politics, I am unfit by intellect and temper for a leading rôle. I was intended, I fear, for a subaltern. Yet we have all something to command, Mr. Fritz, if it be only our own temper; and a man about to marry must look closely to himself. The husband's, like the prince's, is a very artificial standing; and it is hard to be kind in either. Do you follow that?'

'O yes, I follow that,' replied the young man, sadly chop-fallen over the nature of the information he had elicited; and then brightening up: 'Is it,' he ventured, 'is it for an arsenal that you have bought the farm?'

'We'll see about that,' the Prince answered, laughing. 'You must not be too zealous. And in the meantime, if I were you, I would say nothing on the subject.'

'O, trust me, sir, for that,' cried Fritz, as he pocketed a crown. 'And you've let nothing out; for I suspected—I might say I knew it—from the first. And mind you, when a guide is required,' he added, 'I know all the forest paths.'

Otto rode away, chuckling. This talk with Fritz had vastly entertained him; nor was he altogether discontented with his bearing at the farm; men, he was able to tell himself, had behaved worse under smaller provocation. And, to harmonise all, the road and the April air were both delightful to his soul.

Up and down, and to and fro, ever mounting through the wooded foothills, the broad white high-road wound onward into Grünewald. On either hand the pines stood coolly rooted—green moss prospering, springs welling forth between their knuckled spurs; and though some were broad and stalwart, and others spiry and slender, yet all stood firm in the same attitude and with the same expression, like a silent army presenting arms.

The road lay all the way apart from towns and villages, which it left on either hand. Here and there, indeed, in the bottom of green glens, the Prince could spy a few congregated roofs, or perhaps above him, on a shoulder, the solitary cabin of a woodman. But the highway was an international undertaking and with its face set for distant cities, scorned the little life of Grünewald. Hence it was exceeding solitary. Near the frontier Otto met a detachment of his own troops marching in the hot dust; and he was recognised and somewhat feebly cheered as he rode by. But from that time forth and for a long while he was alone with the great woods.

Gradually the spell of pleasure relaxed; his own thoughts returned, like stinging insects, in a cloud; and the talk of the night before, like a shower of buffets, fell upon his memory. He looked east and west for any comforter; and presently he was aware of a cross-road coming steeply down hill, and a horseman cautiously descending. A human voice or presence, like a spring in the desert, was now welcome in itself, and Otto drew bridle to await the coming of this stranger. He proved to be a very red-faced, thick-lipped countryman, with a pair of fat saddle-bags and a stone bottle at his waist; who, as soon as the Prince hailed him, jovially, if somewhat thickly, answered. At the same time he gave a beery yaw in the saddle. It was clear his bottle was no longer full.

'Do you ride towards Mittwalden?' asked the Prince.

'As far as the cross-road to Tannenbrunn,' the man replied. 'Will you bear company?'

'With pleasure. I have even waited for you on the chance,' answered Otto.

By this time they were close alongside; and the man, with the countryfolk instinct, turned his cloudy vision first of all on his companion's mount. 'The devil!' he cried. 'You ride a bonny mare, friend!' And then, his curiosity being satisfied about the essential, he turned his attention to that merely secondary matter, his companion's face. He started. 'The Prince!' he cried, saluting, with another yaw that came near dismounting him. 'I beg your pardon, your Highness, not to have recognised you at once.'

The Prince was vexed out of his self-possession. 'Since you know me,' he said, 'it is unnecessary we should ride together. I will precede you, if you please.' And he was about to set spur to the grey mare, when the half-drunken fellow, reaching over, laid his hand upon the rein.

'Hark you,' he said, 'prince or no prince, that is not how one man should conduct himself with another. What! You'll ride with me incog. and set me talking! But if I know you, you'll preshede me, if you please! Spy!' And the fellow, crimson with drink and injured vanity, almost spat the word into the Prince's face.

A horrid confusion came over Otto. He perceived that he had acted rudely, grossly presuming on his station. And perhaps a little shiver of physical alarm mingled with his remorse, for the fellow was very powerful and not more than half in the possession of his senses. 'Take your hand from my rein,' he said, with a sufficient assumption of command; and when the man, rather to his wonder, had obeyed: 'You should understand, sir,' he added, 'that while I might be glad to ride with you as one person of sagacity with another, and so receive your true opinions, it would amuse me very little to hear the empty compliments you would address to me as Prince.'

'You think I would lie, do you?' cried the man with the bottle, purpling deeper.

'I know you would,' returned Otto, entering entirely into his self-possession. 'You would not even show me the medal you wear about your neck.' For he had caught a glimpse of a green ribbon at the fellow's throat.

The change was instantaneous: the red face became mottled with yellow: a thick-fingered, tottering hand made a clutch at the tell-tale ribbon. 'Medal!' the man cried, wonderfully sobered. 'I have no medal.'

'Pardon me,' said the Prince. 'I will even tell you what that medal bears: a Phoenix burning, with the word *Libertas*.' The medallist remaining speechless, 'You are a pretty fellow,' continued Otto, smiling, 'to complain of incivility from the man whom you conspire to murder.'

'Murder!' protested the man. 'Nay, never that; nothing criminal for me!'

'You are strangely misinformed,' said Otto. 'Conspiracy itself is criminal, and ensures the pain of death. Nay, sir, death it is; I will guarantee my accuracy. Not that you need be so deplorably affected, for I am no officer. But those who mingle with politics should look at both sides of the medal.'

'Your Highness . . . ' began the knight of the bottle.

'Nonsense! you are a Republican,' cried Otto; 'what have you to do with highnesses? But let us continue to ride forward. Since you so much desire it, I cannot find it in my heart to deprive you of my company. And for that matter, I have a question to address to you. Why, being so great a body of men—for you are a great body—fifteen thousand, I have heard, but that will be understated; am I right?'

The man gurgled in his throat.

'Why, then, being so considerable a party,' resumed Otto, 'do you not come before me boldly with your wants?—what do I say? with your commands? Have I the name of being passionately devoted to my throne? I can scarce suppose it. Come, then; show me your majority, and I will instantly resign. Tell this to your friends; assure them from me of my docility; assure them that, however they conceive of my deficiencies, they cannot suppose me more unfit to be a ruler than I do myself. I am one of the worst princes in Europe; will they improve on that?'

'Far be it from me . . .' the man began.

'See, now, if you will not defend my government!' cried Otto. 'If I were you, I would leave conspiracies. You are as little fit to be a conspirator as I to be a king.'

'One thing I will say out,' said the man. 'It is not so much you that we complain of, it's your lady.'

'Not a word, sir' said the Prince; and then after a moment's pause, and in tones of some anger and contempt: 'I once more advise you to have done with politics,' he added; 'and when next I see you, let me see you sober. A morning drunkard is the last man to sit in judgment even upon the worst of princes.'

'I have had a drop, but I had not been drinking,' the man replied, triumphing in a sound distinction. 'And if I had, what then? Nobody hangs by me. But my mill is standing idle, and I blame it on your wife. Am I alone in that? Go round and ask. Where are the mills? Where are the young men that should be working? Where is the currency? All paralysed. No, sir, it is not equal; for I suffer for your faults—I pay for them, by George, out of a poor man's pocket. And what have you to do with mine? Drunk or sober, I can see my country going to hell, and I can see whose fault it is. And so now, I've said my say, and you may drag me to a stinking dungeon; what care I? I've spoke the truth, and so I'll hold hard, and not intrude upon your Highness's society.'

And the miller reined up and, clumsily enough, saluted.

'You will observe, I have not asked your name,' said Otto. 'I wish you a good ride,' and he rode on hard. But let him ride as he pleased, this interview with the miller was a chokepear, which he could not swallow. He had begun by receiving a reproof in manners, and ended by sustaining a defeat in logic, both from a man whom he despised. All his old thoughts returned with fresher venom. And by three in the afternoon, coming to the cross-roads for Beckstein, Otto decided to turn aside and dine there leisurely. Nothing at least could be worse than to go on as he was going.

In the inn at Beckstein he remarked, immediately upon his entrance, an intelligent young gentleman dining, with a book in front of him. He had his own place laid close to the reader, and with a proper apology, broke ground by asking what he read.

'I am perusing,' answered the young gentleman, 'the last work of the Herr Doctor Hohenstockwitz, cousin and librarian of your Prince here in Grünewald—a man of great erudition and some lambencies of wit.'

'I am acquainted,' said Otto, 'with the Herr Doctor, though not yet with his work.'

'Two privileges that I must envy you,' replied the young man politely: 'an honour in hand, a pleasure in the bush.'

'The Herr Doctor is a man much respected, I believe, for his attainments?' asked the Prince.

'He is, sir, a remarkable instance of the force of intellect,' replied the reader. 'Who of our young men know anything of his cousin, all reigning Prince although he be? Who but has heard of Doctor Gotthold? But intellectual merit, alone of all distinctions, has its base in nature.'

'I have the gratification of addressing a student—perhaps an author?' Otto suggested.

The young man somewhat flushed. 'I have some claim to both distinctions, sir, as you suppose,' said he; 'there is my card. I am the licentiate Roederer, author of several works on the theory and practice of politics.'

'You immensely interest me,' said the Prince; 'the more so as I gather that here in Grünewald we are on the brink of revolution. Pray, since these have been your special studies, would you augur hopefully of such a movement?'

'I perceive,' said the young author, with a certain vinegary twitch, 'that you are unacquainted with my opuscula. I am a convinced authoritarian. I share none of those illusory, Utopian fancies with which empirics blind themselves and exasperate the ignorant. The day of these ideas is, believe me, past, or at least passing.'

'When I look about me—' began Otto.

'When you look about you,' interrupted the licentiate, 'you behold the ignorant. But in the laboratory of opinion, beside the studious lamp, we begin already to discard these figments. We begin to return to nature's order, to what I might call, if I were to borrow from the language of therapeutics, the expectant treatment of abuses. You will not misunderstand me,' he continued: 'a country in the condition in which we find Grünewald, a prince such as your Prince Otto, we must explicitly condemn; they are behind the age. But I would look for a remedy not to brute convulsions, but to the natural supervenience of a more able sovereign. I should amuse you, perhaps,' added the licentiate, with a smile, 'I think I should amuse you if I were to explain my notion of a prince. We who have studied in the closet, no longer, in this age, propose ourselves for active service. The paths, we have perceived, are incompatible. I would not have a student on the throne, though I would have one near by for an adviser. I would set forward as prince a man of a good, medium understanding, lively rather than deep; a man of courtly manner, possessed of the double art to ingratiate and to command; receptive, accommodating, seductive. I have been observing you since your first entrance. Well, sir, were I a subject of Grünewald I should pray heaven to set upon the seat of government just such another as yourself.'

'The devil you would!' exclaimed the Prince.

The licentiate Roederer laughed most heartily. 'I thought I should astonish you,' he said. 'These are not the ideas of the masses.'

'They are not, I can assure you,' Otto said.

'Or rather,' distinguished the licentiate, 'not to-day. The time will come, however, when these ideas shall prevail.'

'You will permit me, sir, to doubt it,' said Otto.

'Modesty is always admirable,' chuckled the theorist. 'But yet I assure you, a man like you, with such a man as, say, Doctor Gotthold at your elbow, would be, for all practical issues, my ideal ruler.'

At this rate the hours sped pleasantly for Otto. But the licentiate unfortunately slept that night at Beckstein, where he was, being dainty in the saddle and given to half stages. And to find a convoy to Mittwalden, and thus mitigate the company of his own thoughts, the Prince had to make favour with a certain party of wood-merchants from various states of the empire, who had been drinking together somewhat noisily at the far end of the apartment.

The night had already fallen when they took the saddle. The merchants were very loud and mirthful; each had a face like a nor'west moon; and they played pranks with each others' horses, and mingled songs and choruses, and alternately remembered and forgot the companion of their ride. Otto thus combined society and solitude, hearkening now to their chattering and empty talk, now to the voices of the encircling forest. The starlit dark, the faint wood airs, the clank of the horse-shoes making broken music, accorded together and attuned his mind. And he was still in a most equal temper when the party reached the top of that long hill that overlooks Mittwalden.

Down in the bottom of a bowl of forest, the lights of the little formal town glittered in a pattern, street crossing street; away by itself on the right, the palace was glowing like a factory.

Although he knew not Otto, one of the wood-merchants was a native of the state. 'There,' said he, pointing to the palace with his whip, 'there is Jezebel's inn.'

'What, do you call it that?' cried another, laughing.

'Ay, that's what they call it,' returned the Grünewalder; and he broke into a song, which the rest, as people well acquainted with the words and air, instantly took up in chorus. Her Serene Highness Amalia Seraphina, Princess of Grünewald, was the heroine, Gondremark the hero of this ballad. Shame hissed in Otto's ears. He reined up short and sat stunned in the saddle; and the singers continued to descend the hill without him.

The song went to a rough, swashing, popular air; and long after the words became inaudible the swing of the music, rising and falling, echoed insult in the Prince's brain. He fled the sounds. Hard by him on his right a road struck towards the palace, and he followed it through the thick shadows and branching alleys of the park. It was a busy place on a fine summer's afternoon, when the court and burghers met and saluted; but at that hour of the night in the early spring it was deserted to the roosting birds. Hares rustled among the covert; here and there a statue stood glimmering, with its eternal gesture; here and there the echo of an imitation temple clattered ghostly to the trampling of the mare. Ten minutes brought him to the upper end of his own home garden, where the small stables opened, over a bridge, upon the park. The yard clock was striking the hour of ten; so was the big bell in the palace bell-tower; and, farther off, the belfries of the town. About the stable all else was silent but the stamping of stalled horses and the rattle of halters. Otto dismounted; and as he did so a memory came back to him: a whisper of dishonest grooms and stolen corn, once heard, long forgotten, and now recurring in the nick of opportunity. He crossed the bridge, and, going up to a window, knocked six or seven heavy blows in a particular cadence, and, as he did so, smiled. Presently a wicket was opened in the gate, and a man's head appeared in the dim starlight.

'Nothing to-night,' said a voice.

'Bring a lantern,' said the Prince.

'Dear heart a' mercy!' cried the groom. 'Who's that?'

'It is I, the Prince,' replied Otto. 'Bring a lantern, take in the mare, and let me through into the garden.'

The man remained silent for a while, his head still projecting through the wicket.

'His Highness!' he said at last. 'And why did your Highness knock so strange?'

'It is a superstition in Mittwalden,' answered Otto, 'that it cheapens corn.'

With a sound like a sob the groom fled. He was very white when he returned, even by the light of the lantern; and his hand trembled as he undid the fastenings and took the mare.

'Your Highness,' he began at last, 'for God's sake . . . ' And there he paused, oppressed with guilt.

'For God's sake, what?' asked Otto cheerfully. 'For God's sake let us have cheaper corn, say I. Good-night!' And he strode off into the garden, leaving the groom petrified once more.

The garden descended by a succession of stone terraces to the level of the fish-pond. On the far side the ground rose again, and was crowned by the confused roofs and gables of the palace. The modern pillared front, the ball-room, the great library, the princely apartments, the busy and illuminated quarters of that great house, all faced the town. The garden side was much older; and here it was almost dark; only a few windows quietly lighted at various elevations. The great square tower rose, thinning by stages like a telescope; and on the top of all the flag hung motionless.

The garden, as it now lay in the dusk and glimmer of the starshine, breathed of April violets. Under night's cavern arch the shrubs obscurely bustled. Through the plotted terraces and down the marble stairs the Prince rapidly descended, fleeing before uncomfortable thoughts. But, alas! from these there is no city of refuge. And now, when he was about midway of the descent, distant strains of music began to fall upon his ear from the ball-room, where the court was dancing. They reached him faint and broken, but they touched the keys of memory; and through and above them Otto heard the ranting melody of the wood-merchants' song. Mere blackness seized upon his mind. Here he was, coming home; the wife was dancing, the husband had been playing a trick upon a lackey; and meanwhile, all about them, they were a by-word to their subjects. Such a prince, such a husband, such a man, as this Otto had become! And he sped the faster onward.

Some way below he came unexpectedly upon a sentry; yet a little farther, and he was challenged by a second; and as he crossed the bridge over the fish-pond, an officer making the rounds stopped him once more. The parade of watch was more than usual; but curiosity was dead in Otto's mind, and he only chafed at the interruption. The porter of the back postern admitted him, and started to behold him so disordered. Thence, hasting by private stairs and passages, he came at length unseen to his own chamber, tore off his clothes, and threw himself upon his bed in the dark. The music of the ball-room still continued to a very lively measure; and still, behind that, he heard in spirit the chorus of the merchants clanking down the hill.

BOOK II
OF LOVE AND POLITICS

CHAPTER I
WHAT HAPPENED IN THE LIBRARY

At a quarter before six on the following morning Doctor Gotthold was already at his desk in the library; and with a small cup of black coffee at his elbow, and an eye occasionally wandering to the busts and the long array of many-coloured books, was quietly reviewing the labours of the day before. He was a man of about forty, flaxen-haired, with refined features a little worn, and bright eyes somewhat faded. Early to bed and early to rise, his life was devoted to two things: erudition and Rhine wine. An ancient friendship existed latent between him and Otto; they rarely met, but when they did it was to take up at once the thread of their suspended intimacy. Gotthold, the virgin priest of knowledge, had envied his cousin, for half a day, when he was married; he had never envied him his throne.

Reading was not a popular diversion at the court of Grünewald; and that great, pleasant, sunshiny gallery of books and statues was, in practice, Gotthold's private cabinet. On this particular Wednesday morning, however, he had not been long about his manuscript when a door opened and the Prince stepped into the apartment. The doctor watched him as he drew near, receiving, from each of the embayed windows in succession, a flush of morning sun; and Otto looked so gay, and walked so airily, he was so well dressed and brushed and frizzled, so point-device, and of such a sovereign elegance, that the heart of his cousin the recluse was rather moved against him.

'Good-morning, Gotthold,' said Otto, dropping in a chair.

'Good-morning, Otto,' returned the librarian. 'You are an early bird. Is this an accident, or do you begin reforming?'

'It is about time, I fancy,' answered the Prince.

'I cannot imagine,' said the Doctor. 'I am too sceptical to be an ethical adviser; and as for good resolutions, I believed in them when I was young. They are the colours of hope's rainbow.'

'If you come to think of it,' said Otto, 'I am not a popular sovereign.' And with a look he changed his statement to a question.

'Popular? Well, there I would distinguish,' answered Gotthold, leaning back and joining the tips of his fingers. 'There are various kinds of popularity; the bookish, which is perfectly impersonal, as unreal as the nightmare; the politician's, a mixed variety; and yours, which is the most personal of all. Women take to you; footmen adore you; it is as natural to like you as to pat a dog; and were you a saw-miller you would be the most popular citizen in Grünewald. As a prince—well, you are in the wrong trade. It is perhaps philosophical to recognise it as you do.'

'Perhaps philosophical?' repeated Otto.

'Yes, perhaps. I would not be dogmatic,' answered Gotthold.

'Perhaps philosophical, and certainly not virtuous,' Otto resumed.

'Not of a Roman virtue,' chuckled the recluse.

Otto drew his chair nearer to the table, leaned upon it with his elbow, and looked his cousin squarely in the face. 'In short,' he asked, 'not manly?'

'Well,' Gotthold hesitated, 'not manly, if you will.' And then, with a laugh, 'I did not know that you gave yourself out to be manly,' he added. 'It was one of the points that I inclined to like about you; inclined, I believe, to admire. The names of virtues exercise a charm on most of us; we must lay claim to all of them, however incompatible; we must all be both daring and prudent; we must all vaunt our pride and go to the stake for our humility. Not so you. Without compromise you were yourself: a pretty sight. I have always said it: none so void of all pretence as Otto.'

'Pretence and effort both!' cried Otto. 'A dead dog in a canal is more alive. And the question, Gotthold, the question that I have to face is this: Can I not, with effort and self-denial, can I not become a tolerable sovereign?'

'Never,' replied Gotthold. 'Dismiss the notion. And besides, dear child, you would not try.'

'Nay, Gotthold, I am not to be put by,' said Otto. 'If I am constitutionally unfit to be a sovereign, what am I doing with this money, with this palace, with these guards? And I—a thief—am to execute the law on others?'

'I admit the difficulty,' said Gotthold.

'Well, can I not try?' continued Otto. 'Am I not bound to try? And with the advice and help of such a man as you—'

'Me!' cried the librarian. 'Now, God forbid!'

Otto, though he was in no very smiling humour, could not forbear to smile. 'Yet I was told last night,' he laughed, 'that with a man like me to impersonate, and a man like you to touch the springs, a very possible government could be composed.'

'Now I wonder in what diseased imagination,' Gotthold said, 'that preposterous monster saw the light of day?'

'It was one of your own trade—a writer: one Roederer,' said Otto.

'Roederer! an ignorant puppy!' cried the librarian.

'You are ungrateful,' said Otto. 'He is one of your professed admirers.'

'Is he?' cried Gotthold, obviously impressed. 'Come, that is a good account of the young man. I must read his stuff again. It is the rather to his credit, as our views are opposite. The east and west are not more opposite. Can I have converted him? But no; the incident belongs to Fairyland.'

'You are not then,' asked the Prince, 'an authoritarian?'

'I? God bless me, no!' said Gotthold. 'I am a red, dear child.'

'That brings me then to my next point, and by a natural transition. If I am so clearly unfitted for my post,' the Prince asked; 'if my friends admit it, if my subjects clamour for my downfall, if revolution is preparing at this hour, must I not go forth to meet the inevitable? should I not save these horrors and be done with these absurdities? in a word, should I not abdicate? O, believe me, I feel the ridicule, the vast abuse of language,' he added, wincing, 'but even a principulus like me cannot resign; he must make a great gesture, and come buskined forth, and abdicate.'

'Ay,' said Gotthold, 'or else stay where he is. What gnat has bitten you to-day? Do you not know that you are touching, with lay hands, the very holiest inwards of philosophy, where madness dwells? Ay, Otto, madness; for in the serene temples of the wise, the inmost shrine, which we carefully keep locked, is full of spiders' webs. All men, all, are fundamentally useless; nature tolerates, she does not need, she does not use them: sterile flowers! All—down to the fellow swinking in a byre, whom fools point out for the exception—all are useless; all weave ropes of sand; or like a child that has breathed on a window, write and obliterate, write and obliterate, idle words! Talk of it no more. That way, I tell you, madness lies.' The speaker rose from his chair and then sat down again. He laughed a little laugh, and then, changing his tone, resumed: 'Yes, dear child, we are not here to do battle with giants; we are here to be happy like the flowers, if we can be. It is because you could, that I have always secretly admired you. Cling to that trade; believe me, it is the right one. Be happy, be idle, be airy. To the devil with all casuistry! and leave the state to Gondremark, as heretofore. He does it well enough, they say; and his vanity enjoys the situation.'

'Gotthold,' cried Otto, 'what is this to me? Useless is not the question; I cannot rest at uselessness; I must be useful or I must be noxious—one or other. I grant you the whole thing, prince and principality alike, is pure absurdity, a stroke of satire; and that a banker or the man who keeps an inn has graver duties. But now, when I have washed my hands of it three years, and left all—labour, responsibility, and honour and enjoyment too, if there be any—to Gondremark and to—Seraphina—' He hesitated at the name, and Gotthold glanced aside. 'Well,' the Prince continued, 'what has come of it? Taxes, army, cannon—why, it's like a box of lead soldiers! And the people sick at the folly of it, and fired with the injustice! And war, too—I hear of war—war in this teapot! What a complication of absurdity and disgrace! And when the inevitable end arrives—the revolution—who will be to blame in the sight of God, who will be gibbeted in public opinion? I! Prince Puppet!'

'I thought you had despised public opinion,' said Gotthold.

'I did,' said Otto sombrely, 'but now I do not. I am growing old. And then, Gotthold, there is Seraphina. She is loathed in this country that I brought her to and suffered her to spoil. Yes, I gave it her as a plaything, and she has broken it: a fine Prince, an admirable Princess! Even her life— I ask you, Gotthold, is her life safe?'

'It is safe enough to-day,' replied the librarian: 'but since you ask me seriously, I would not answer for to-morrow. She is ill-advised.'

'And by whom? By this Gondremark, to whom you counsel me to leave my country,' cried the Prince. 'Rare advice! The course that I have been following all these years, to come at last to this. O, ill-advised! if that were all! See now, there is no sense in beating about the bush between two men: you know what scandal says of her?'

Gotthold, with pursed lips, silently nodded.

'Well, come, you are not very cheering as to my conduct as the Prince; have I even done my duty as a husband?' Otto asked.

'Nay, nay,' said Gotthold, earnestly and eagerly, 'this is another chapter. I am an old celibate, an old monk. I cannot advise you in your marriage.'

'Nor do I require advice,' said Otto, rising. 'All of this must cease.' And he began to walk to and fro with his hands behind his back.

'Well, Otto, may God guide you!' said Gotthold, after a considerable silence. 'I cannot.'

'From what does all this spring?' said the Prince, stopping in his walk. 'What am I to call it? Diffidence? The fear of ridicule? Inverted vanity? What matter names, if it has brought me to this? I could never bear to be bustling about nothing; I was ashamed of this toy kingdom from the first; I could not tolerate that people should fancy I believed in a thing so patently absurd! I would do nothing that cannot be done smiling. I have a sense of humour, forsooth! I must know better than my Maker. And it was the same thing in my marriage,' he added more hoarsely. 'I did not believe this girl could care for me; I must not intrude; I must preserve the foppery of my indifference. What an impotent picture!'

'Ay, we have the same blood,' moralised Gotthold. 'You are drawing, with fine strokes, the character of the born sceptic.'

'Sceptic?—coward!' cried Otto. 'Coward is the word. A springless, putty-hearted, cowering coward!'

And as the Prince rapped out the words in tones of unusual vigour, a little, stout, old gentleman, opening a door behind Gotthold, received them fairly in the face. With his parrot's beak for a nose, his pursed mouth, his little goggling eyes, he was the picture of formality; and in ordinary circumstances, strutting behind the drum of his corporation, he impressed the beholder with a certain air of frozen dignity and wisdom. But at the smallest contrariety, his trembling hands and disconnected gestures betrayed the weakness at the root. And now, when he was thus surprisingly received in that library of Mittwalden Palace, which was the customary haunt of silence, his hands went up into the air as if he had been shot, and he cried aloud with the scream of an old woman.

'O!' he gasped, recovering, 'Your Highness! I beg ten thousand pardons. But your Highness at such an hour in the library!—a circumstance so unusual as your Highness's presence was a thing I could not be expected to foresee.'

'There is no harm done, Herr Cancellarius,' said Otto.

'I came upon the errand of a moment: some papers I left over-night with the Herr Doctor,' said the Chancellor of Grünewald. 'Herr Doctor, if you will kindly give me them, I will intrude no longer.'

Gotthold unlocked a drawer and handed a bundle of manuscript to the old gentleman, who prepared, with fitting salutations, to take his departure.

'Herr Greisengesang, since we have met,' said Otto, 'let us talk.'

'I am honoured by his Highness's commands,' replied the Chancellor.

'All has been quiet since I left?' asked the Prince, resuming his seat.

'The usual business, your Highness,' answered Greisengesang; 'punctual trifles: huge, indeed, if neglected, but trifles when discharged. Your Highness is most zealously obeyed.'

'Obeyed, Herr Cancellarius?' returned the Prince. 'And when have I obliged you with an order? Replaced, let us rather say. But to touch upon these trifles; instance me a few.'

'The routine of government, from which your Highness has so wisely dissociated his leisure . . . ' began Greisengesang.

'We will leave my leisure, sir,' said Otto. 'Approach the facts.'

'The routine of business was proceeded with,' replied the official, now visibly twittering.

'It is very strange, Herr Cancellarius, that you should so persistently avoid my questions,' said the Prince. 'You tempt me to suppose a purpose in your dulness. I have asked you whether all was quiet; do me the pleasure to reply.'

'Perfectly—O, perfectly quiet,' jerked the ancient puppet, with every signal of untruth.

'I make a note of these words,' said the Prince gravely. 'You assure me, your sovereign, that since the date of my departure nothing has occurred of which you owe me an account.'

'I take your Highness, I take the Herr Doctor to witness,' cried Greisengesang, 'that I have had no such expression.'

'Halt!' said the Prince; and then, after a pause: 'Herr Greisengesang, you are an old man, and you served my father before you served me,' he added. 'It consists neither with your dignity nor mine that you should babble excuses and stumble possibly upon untruths. Collect your thoughts; and then categorically inform me of all you have been charged to hide.'

Gotthold, stooping very low over his desk, appeared to have resumed his labours; but his shoulders heaved with subterranean merriment. The Prince waited, drawing his handkerchief quietly through his fingers.

'Your Highness, in this informal manner,' said the old gentleman at last, 'and being unavoidably deprived of documents, it would be difficult, it would be impossible, to do justice to the somewhat grave occurrences which have transpired.'

'I will not criticise your attitude,' replied the Prince. 'I desire that, between you and me, all should be done gently; for I have not forgotten, my old friend, that you were kind to me from the first, and for a period of years a faithful servant. I will thus dismiss the matters on which you waive immediate inquiry. But you have certain papers actually in your hand. Come, Herr Greisengesang, there is at least one point for which you have authority. Enlighten me on that.'

'On that?' cried the old gentleman. 'O, that is a trifle; a matter, your Highness, of police; a detail of a purely administrative order. These are simply a selection of the papers seized upon the English traveller.'

'Seized?' echoed Otto. 'In what sense? Explain yourself.'

'Sir John Crabtree,' interposed Gotthold, looking up, 'was arrested yesterday evening.'

'It this so, Herr Cancellarius?' demanded Otto sternly.

'It was judged right, your Highness,' protested Greisengesang. 'The decree was in due form, invested with your Highness's authority by procuration. I am but an agent; I had no status to prevent the measure.'

'This man, my guest, has been arrested,' said the Prince. 'On what grounds, sir? With what colour of pretence?'

The Chancellor stammered.

'Your Highness will perhaps find the reason in these documents,' said Gotthold, pointing with the tail of his pen.

Otto thanked his cousin with a look. 'Give them to me,' he said, addressing the Chancellor.

But that gentleman visibly hesitated to obey. 'Baron von Gondremark,' he said, 'has made the affair his own. I am in this case a mere messenger; and as such, I am not clothed with any capacity to communicate the documents I carry. Herr Doctor, I am convinced you will not fail to bear me out.'

'I have heard a great deal of nonsense,' said Gotthold, 'and most of it from you; but this beats all.'

'Come, sir,' said Otto, rising, 'the papers. I command.'

Herr Greisengesang instantly gave way.

'With your Highness's permission,' he said, 'and laying at his feet my most submiss apologies, I will now hasten to attend his further orders in the Chancery.'

'Herr Cancellarius, do you see this chair?' said Otto. 'There is where you shall attend my further orders. O, now, no more!' he cried, with a gesture, as the old man opened his lips. 'You have sufficiently marked your zeal to your employer; and I begin to weary of a moderation you abuse.'

The Chancellor moved to the appointed chair and took his seat in silence.

'And now,' said Otto, opening the roll, 'what is all this? it looks like the manuscript of a book.'

'It is,' said Gotthold, 'the manuscript of a book of travels.'

'You have read it, Doctor Hohenstockwitz?' asked the Prince.

'Nay, I but saw the title-page,' replied Gotthold. 'But the roll was given to me open, and I heard no word of any secrecy.'

Otto dealt the Chancellor an angry glance.

'I see,' he went on. 'The papers of an author seized at this date of the world's history, in a state so petty and so ignorant as Grünewald, here is indeed an ignominious folly. Sir,' to the Chancellor, 'I marvel to find you in so scurvy an employment. On your conduct to your Prince I will not dwell; but to descend to be a spy! For what else can it be called? To seize the papers of this gentleman, the private papers of a stranger, the toil of a life, perhaps—to open, and to read them. And what have we to do with books? The Herr Doctor might perhaps be asked for his advice; but we have no *index expurgatorius* in Grünewald. Had we but that, we should be the most absolute parody and farce upon this tawdry earth.'

Yet, even while Otto spoke, he had continued to unfold the roll; and now, when it lay fully open, his eye rested on the title-page elaborately written in red ink. It ran thus:

MEMOIRS
OF A VISIT TO THE VARIOUS
COURTS OF EUROPE,
BY
SIR JOHN CRABTREE, BARONET.

Below was a list of chapters, each bearing the name of one of the European Courts; and among these the nineteenth and the last upon the list was dedicated to Grünewald.

'Ah! The Court of Grünewald!' said Otto, 'that should be droll reading.' And his curiosity itched for it.

'A methodical dog, this English Baronet,' said Gotthold. 'Each chapter written and finished on the spot. I shall look for his work when it appears.'

'It would be odd, now, just to glance at it,' said Otto, wavering.

Gotthold's brow darkened, and he looked out of window.

But though the Prince understood the reproof, his weakness prevailed. 'I will,' he said, with an uneasy laugh, 'I will, I think, just glance at it.'

So saying, he resumed his seat and spread the traveller's manuscript upon the table.

CHAPTER II
'ON THE COURT OF GRÜNEWALD,' BEING A PORTION OF THE TRAVELLER'S MANUSCRIPT

It may well be asked (*it was thus the English traveller began his nineteenth chapter*) why I should have chosen Grünewald out of so many other states equally petty, formal, dull, and corrupt. Accident, indeed, decided, and not I; but I have seen no reason to regret my visit. The spectacle of this small society macerating in its own abuses was not perhaps instructive, but I have found it exceedingly diverting.

The reigning Prince, Otto Johann Friedrich, a young man of imperfect education, questionable valour, and no scintilla of capacity, has fallen into entire public contempt. It was with difficulty that I obtained an interview, for he is frequently absent from a court where his presence is unheeded, and where his only rôle is to be a cloak for the amours of his wife. At last, however, on the third occasion when I visited the palace, I found this sovereign in the exercise of his inglorious function, with the wife on one hand, and the lover on the other. He is not ill-looking; he has hair of a ruddy gold, which naturally curls, and his eyes are dark, a combination which I always regard as the mark of some congenital deficiency, physical or moral; his features are irregular, but pleasing; the nose perhaps a little short, and the mouth a little womanish; his address is excellent, and he can express himself with point. But to pierce below these externals is to come on a vacuity of any sterling quality, a deliquescence of the moral nature, a frivolity and inconsequence of purpose that mark the nearly perfect fruit of a decadent age. He has a worthless smattering of many subjects, but a grasp of none. 'I soon weary of a pursuit,' he said to me, laughing; it would almost appear as if he took a pride in his incapacity and lack of moral courage. The results of his dilettanteism are to be seen in every field; he is a bad fencer, a second-rate horseman, dancer, shot; he sings—I have heard him—and he sings like a child; he writes intolerable verses in more than doubtful French; he acts like the common amateur; and in short there is no end to the number of the things that he does, and does badly. His one manly taste is for the chase. In sum, he is but a plexus of weaknesses; the singing chambermaid of the stage, tricked out in man's apparel, and mounted on a circus horse. I have seen this poor phantom of a prince riding out alone or with a few huntsmen, disregarded by all, and I have been even grieved for the bearer of so futile and melancholy an existence. The last Merovingians may have looked not otherwise.

The Princess Amalia Seraphina, a daughter of the Grand-Ducal house of Toggenburg-Tannhäuser, would be equally inconsiderable if she were not a cutting instrument in the hands of an ambitious man. She is much younger than the Prince, a girl of two-and-twenty, sick with vanity, superficially clever, and fundamentally a fool. She has a red-brown rolling eye, too large for her face, and with sparks of both levity and ferocity; her forehead is high and narrow, her figure thin and a little stooping. Her manners, her conversation, which she interlards with French, her very tastes and ambitions, are alike assumed; and the assumption is ungracefully apparent: Hoyden playing Cleopatra. I should judge her to be incapable of truth. In private life a girl of this description embroils the peace of families, walks attended by a troop of scowling swains, and passes, once at least, through the divorce court; it is a common and, except to the cynic, an uninteresting type. On the throne, however, and in the hands of a man like Gondremark, she may become the authoress of serious public evils.

Gondremark, the true ruler of this unfortunate country, is a more complex study. His position in Grünewald, to which he is a foreigner, is eminently false; and that he should maintain it as he does, a very miracle of impudence and dexterity. His speech, his face, his policy, are all double: heads and tails. Which of the two extremes may be his actual design he were a bold man who should offer to decide. Yet I will hazard the guess that he follows both experimentally, and awaits, at the hand of destiny, one of those directing hints of which she is so lavish to the wise.

On the one hand, as *Maire du Palais* to the incompetent Otto, and using the love-sick Princess for a tool and mouthpiece, he pursues a policy of arbitrary power and territorial aggrandisement. He has called out the whole capable male population of the state to military service; he has bought cannon; he has tempted away promising officers from foreign armies; and he now begins, in his international relations, to assume the swaggering port and the vague, threatful language of a bully. The idea of extending Grünewald may appear absurd, but the little state is advantageously placed, its neighbours are all defenceless; and if at any moment the jealousies of the greater courts should neutralise each other, an active policy might double the principality both in population and extent. Certainly at least the scheme is entertained in the court of Mittwalden; nor do I myself regard it as entirely desperate. The margravate of Brandenburg has grown from as small beginnings to a formidable power; and though it is late in the day to try adventurous policies, and the age of war seems ended, Fortune, we must not forget, still blindly turns her wheel for men and nations. Concurrently with, and tributary to, these warlike preparations, crushing taxes have been levied, journals have been suppressed, and the country, which three years ago was prosperous and happy, now stagnates in a forced inaction, gold has become a curiosity, and the mills stand idle on the mountain streams.

On the other hand, in his second capacity of popular tribune, Gondremark is the incarnation of the free lodges, and sits at the centre of an organised conspiracy against the state. To any such movement my sympathies were early acquired, and I would not willingly let fall a word that might embarrass or retard the revolution. But to show that I speak of knowledge, and not as the reporter of mere gossip, I may mention that I have myself been present at a meeting where the details of a republican Constitution were minutely debated and arranged; and I may add that Gondremark was throughout referred to by the speakers as their captain in action and the arbiter of their disputes. He has taught his dupes (for so I must regard them) that his power of resistance to the Princess is limited, and at each fresh stretch of authority persuades them, with specious reasons, to postpone the hour of insurrection. Thus (to give some instances of his astute diplomacy) he salved over the decree enforcing military service, under the plea that to be well drilled and exercised in arms was even a necessary preparation for revolt. And the other day, when it began to be rumoured abroad that a war was being forced on a reluctant neighbour, the Grand Duke of Gerolstein, and I made sure it would be the signal for an instant rising, I was struck dumb with wonder to find that even this had been prepared and was to be accepted. I went from one to another in the Liberal camp, and all were in the same story, all had been drilled and schooled and fitted out with vacuous argument. 'The lads had better see some real fighting,' they said; 'and besides, it will be as well to capture Gerolstein: we can then extend to our neighbours the blessing of liberty on the same day that we snatch it for ourselves; and the republic will be all the stronger to resist, if the kings of Europe should band themselves together to reduce it.' I know not which of the two I should admire the more: the simplicity of the multitude or the audacity of the adventurer. But such are the subtleties, such the quibbling reasons, with which he blinds and leads this people. How long a course so tortuous can be pursued with safety I am incapable of guessing; not long, one would suppose; and yet this singular man has been treading the mazes for five years, and his favour at court and his popularity among the lodges still endure unbroken.

I have the privilege of slightly knowing him. Heavily and somewhat clumsily built, of a vast, disjointed, rambling frame, he can still pull himself together, and figure, not without admiration, in the saloon or the ball-room. His hue and temperament are plentifully bilious; he has a saturnine eye; his cheek is of a dark blue where he has been shaven. Essentially he is to be numbered among the man-haters, a convinced contemner of his fellows. Yet he is himself of a commonplace ambition and greedy of applause. In talk, he is remarkable for a thirst of information, loving rather to hear than to communicate; for sound and studious views; and, judging by the extreme short-sightedness of common politicians, for a remarkable provision of events. All this, however, without grace, pleasantry, or charm, heavily set forth, with a dull countenance. In our numerous conversations, although he has always heard me with deference, I have been conscious throughout of a sort of ponderous finessing hard to tolerate. He produces none of the effect of a gentleman; devoid not merely of pleasantry, but of all attention or communicative warmth of bearing. No gentleman, besides, would so parade his amours with the Princess; still less repay the Prince for his long-suffering with a studied insolence of demeanour and the fabrication of insulting nicknames, such as Prince Featherhead, which run from ear to ear and create a laugh throughout the country. Gondremark has thus some of the clumsier characters of the self-made man, combined with an inordinate, almost a besotted, pride of intellect and birth. Heavy, bilious, selfish, inornate, he sits upon this court and country like an incubus.

But it is probable that he preserves softer gifts for necessary purposes. Indeed, it is certain, although he vouchsafed none of it to me, that this cold and stolid politician possesses to a great degree the art of ingratiation, and can be all things to all men. Hence there has probably sprung up the idle legend that in private life he is a gross romping voluptuary. Nothing, at least, can well be more surprising than the terms of his connection with the Princess. Older than her husband, certainly uglier, and, according to the feeble ideas common among women, in every particular less pleasing, he has not only seized the complete command of all her thought and action, but has imposed on her in public a humiliating part. I do not here refer to the complete sacrifice of every rag of her reputation; for to many women these extremities are in themselves attractive. But there is about the court a certain lady of a dishevelled reputation, a Countess von Rosen, wife or widow of a cloudy count, no longer in her second youth, and already bereft of some of her attractions, who unequivocally occupies the station of the Baron's mistress. I had thought, at first, that she was but a hired accomplice, a mere blind or buffer for the more important sinner. A few hours' acquaintance with Madame von Rosen for ever dispelled the illusion. She is one rather to make than to prevent a scandal, and she values none of those bribes—money, honours, or employment—with which the situation might be gilded. Indeed, as a person frankly bad, she pleased me, in the court of Grünewald, like a piece of nature.

The power of this man over the Princess is, therefore, without bounds. She has sacrificed to the adoration with which he has inspired her not only her marriage vow and every shred of public decency, but that vice of jealousy which is so much dearer to the female sex than either intrinsic honour or outward consideration. Nay, more: a young, although not a very attractive woman, and a princess both by birth and fact, she submits to the triumphant rivalry of one who might be her mother as to years, and who is so manifestly her inferior in station. This is one of the mysteries of the human heart. But the rage of illicit love, when it is once indulged, appears to grow by feeding; and to a person of the character and temperament of this unfortunate young lady, almost any depth of degradation is within the reach of possibility.

CHAPTER III
THE PRINCE AND THE ENGLISH TRAVELLER

So far Otto read, with waxing indignation; and here his fury overflowed. He tossed the roll upon the table and stood up. 'This man,' he said, 'is a devil. A filthy imagination, an ear greedy of evil, a ponderous malignity of thought and language: I grow like him by the reading! Chancellor, where is this fellow lodged?'

'He was committed to the Flag Tower,' replied Greisengesang, 'in the Gamiani apartment.'

'Lead me to him,' said the Prince; and then, a thought striking him, 'Was it for that,' he asked, 'that I found so many sentries in the garden?'

'Your Highness, I am unaware,' answered Greisengesang, true to his policy. 'The disposition of the guards is a matter distinct from my functions.'

Otto turned upon the old man fiercely, but ere he had time to speak, Gotthold touched him on the arm. He swallowed his wrath with a great effort. 'It is well,' he said, taking the roll. 'Follow me to the Flag Tower.'

The Chancellor gathered himself together, and the two set forward. It was a long and complicated voyage; for the library was in the wing of the new buildings, and the tower which carried the flag was in the old schloss upon the garden. By a great variety of stairs and corridors, they came out at last upon a patch of gravelled court; the garden peeped through a high grating with a flash of green; tall, old gabled buildings mounted on every side; the Flag Tower climbed, stage after stage, into the blue; and high over all, among the building daws, the yellow flag wavered in the wind. A sentinel at the foot of the tower stairs presented arms; another paced the first landing; and a third was stationed before the door of the extemporised prison.

'We guard this mud-bag like a jewel,' Otto sneered.

The Gamiani apartment was so called from an Italian doctor who had imposed on the credulity of a former prince. The rooms were large, airy, pleasant, and looked upon the garden; but the walls were of great thickness (for the tower was old), and the windows were heavily barred. The Prince, followed by the Chancellor, still trotting to keep up with him, brushed swiftly through the little library and the long saloon, and burst like a thunderbolt into the bedroom at the farther end. Sir John was finishing his toilet; a man of fifty, hard, uncompromising, able, with the eye and teeth of physical courage. He was unmoved by the irruption, and bowed with a sort of sneering ease.

'To what am I to attribute the honour of this visit?' he asked.

'You have eaten my bread,' replied Otto, 'you have taken my hand, you have been received under my roof. When did I fail you in courtesy? What have you asked that was not granted as to an honoured guest? And here, sir,' tapping fiercely on the manuscript, 'here is your return.'

'Your Highness has read my papers?' said the Baronet. 'I am honoured indeed. But the sketch is most imperfect. I shall now have much to add. I can say that the Prince, whom I had accused of idleness, is zealous in the department of police, taking upon himself those duties that are most distasteful. I shall be able to relate the burlesque incident of my arrest, and the singular interview with which you honour me at present. For the rest, I have already communicated with my Ambassador at Vienna; and unless you propose to murder me, I shall be at liberty, whether you please or not, within the week. For I hardly fancy the future empire of Grünewald is yet ripe to go to war with England. I conceive I am a little more than quits. I owe you no explanation; yours has been the wrong. You, if you have studied my writing with intelligence, owe me a large debt of gratitude. And to conclude, as I have not yet finished my toilet, I imagine the courtesy of a turnkey to a prisoner would induce you to withdraw.'

There was some paper on the table, and Otto, sitting down, wrote a passport in the name of Sir John Crabtree.

'Affix the seal, Herr Cancellarius,' he said, in his most princely manner, as he rose.

Greisengesang produced a red portfolio, and affixed the seal in the unpoetic guise of an adhesive stamp; nor did his perturbed and clumsy movements at all lessen the comedy of the performance. Sir John looked on with a malign enjoyment; and Otto chafed, regretting, when too late, the unnecessary royalty of his command and gesture. But at length the Chancellor had finished his piece of prestidigitation, and, without waiting for an order, had countersigned the passport. Thus regularised, he returned it to Otto with a bow.

'You will now,' said the Prince, 'order one of my own carriages to be prepared; see it, with your own eyes, charged with Sir John's effects, and have it waiting within the hour behind the Pheasant House. Sir John departs this morning for Vienna.'

The Chancellor took his elaborate departure.

'Here, sir, is your passport,' said Otto, turning to the Baronet. 'I regret it from my heart that you have met inhospitable usage.'

'Well, there will be no English war,' returned Sir John.

'Nay, sir,' said Otto, 'you surely owe me your civility. Matters are now changed, and we stand again upon the footing of two gentlemen. It was not I who ordered your arrest; I returned late last night from hunting; and as you cannot blame me for your imprisonment, you may even thank me for your freedom.'

'And yet you read my papers,' said the traveller shrewdly.

'There, sir, I was wrong,' returned Otto; 'and for that I ask your pardon. You can scarce refuse it, for your own dignity, to one who is a plexus of weaknesses. Nor was the fault entirely mine. Had the papers been innocent, it would have been at most an indiscretion. Your own guilt is the sting of my offence.'

Sir John regarded Otto with an approving twinkle; then he bowed, but still in silence.

'Well, sir, as you are now at your entire disposal, I have a favour to beg of your indulgence,' continued the Prince. 'I have to request that you will walk with me alone into the garden so soon as your convenience permits.'

'From the moment that I am a free man,' Sir John replied, this time with perfect courtesy, 'I am wholly at your Highness's command; and if you will excuse a rather summary toilet, I will even follow you, as I am.'

'I thank you, sir,' said Otto.

So without more delay, the Prince leading, the pair proceeded down through the echoing stairway of the tower, and out through the grating, into the ample air and sunshine of the morning, and among the terraces and flower-beds of the garden. They crossed the fish-pond, where the carp were leaping as thick as bees; they mounted, one after another, the various flights of stairs, snowed upon, as they went, with April blossoms, and marching in time to the great orchestra of birds. Nor did Otto pause till they had reached the highest terrace of the garden. Here was a gate into the park, and hard by, under a tuft of laurel, a marble garden seat. Hence they looked down on the green tops of many elm-trees, where the rooks were busy; and, beyond that, upon the palace roof, and the yellow banner flying in the blue. I pray you to be seated, sir,' said Otto.

Sir John complied without a word; and for some seconds Otto walked to and fro before him, plunged in angry thought. The birds were all singing for a wager.

'Sir,' said the Prince at length, turning towards the Englishman, 'you are to me, except by the conventions of society, a perfect stranger. Of your character and wishes I am ignorant. I have never wittingly disobliged you. There is a difference in station, which I desire to waive. I would, if you still think me entitled to so much consideration—I would be regarded simply as a gentleman. Now, sir, I did wrong to glance at these papers, which I here return to you; but if curiosity be undignified, as I am free to own, falsehood is both cowardly and cruel. I opened your roll; and what did I find—what did I find about my wife; Lies!' he broke out. 'They are lies! There are not, so help me God! four words of truth in your intolerable libel! You are a man; you are old, and might be the girl's father; you are a gentleman; you are a scholar, and have learned refinement; and you rake together all this vulgar scandal, and propose to print it in a public book! Such is your chivalry! But, thank God, sir, she has still a husband. You say, sir, in that paper in your hand, that I am a bad fencer; I have to request from you a lesson in the art. The park is close behind; yonder is the Pheasant House, where you will find your carriage; should I fall, you know, sir—you have written it in your paper—how little my movements are regarded; I am in the custom of disappearing; it will be one more disappearance; and long before it has awakened a remark, you may be safe across the border.'

'You will observe,' said Sir John, 'that what you ask is impossible.'

'And if I struck you?' cried the Prince, with a sudden menacing flash.

'It would be a cowardly blow,' returned the Baronet, unmoved, 'for it would make no change. I cannot draw upon a reigning sovereign.'

'And it is this man, to whom you dare not offer satisfaction, that you choose to insult!' cried Otto.

'Pardon me,' said the traveller, 'you are unjust. It is because you are a reigning sovereign that I cannot fight with you; and it is for the same reason that I have a right to criticise your action and your wife. You are in everything a public creature; you belong to the public, body and bone. You have with you the law, the muskets of the army, and the eyes of spies. We, on our side, have but one weapon—truth.'

'Truth!' echoed the Prince, with a gesture.

There was another silence.

'Your Highness,' said Sir John at last, 'you must not expect grapes from a thistle. I am old and a cynic. Nobody cares a rush for me; and on the whole, after the present interview, I scarce know anybody that I like better than yourself. You see, I have changed my mind, and have the uncommon virtue to avow the change. I tear up this stuff before you, here in your own garden; I ask your pardon, I ask the pardon of the Princess; and I give you my word of honour as a gentleman and an old man, that when my book of travels shall appear it shall not contain so much as the name of Grünewald. And yet it was a racy chapter! But had your Highness only read about the other courts! I am a carrion crow; but it is not my fault, after all, that the world is such a nauseous kennel.'

'Sir,' said Otto, 'is the eye not jaundiced?'

'Nay,' cried the traveller, 'very likely. I am one who goes sniffing; I am no poet. I believe in a better future for the world; or, at all accounts, I do most potently disbelieve in the present. Rotten eggs is the burthen of my song. But indeed, your Highness, when I meet with any merit, I do not think that I am slow to recognise it. This is a day that I shall still recall with gratitude, for I have found a sovereign with some manly virtues; and for once—old courtier and old radical as I am—it is from the heart and quite sincerely that I can request the honour of kissing your Highness's hand?'

'Nay, sir,' said Otto, 'to my heart!'

And the Englishman, taken at unawares, was clasped for a moment in the Prince's arms.

'And now, sir,' added Otto, 'there is the Pheasant House; close behind it you will find my carriage, which I pray you to accept. God speed you to Vienna!'

'In the impetuosity of youth,' replied Sir John, 'your Highness has overlooked one circumstance. I am still fasting.'

'Well, sir,' said Otto, smiling, 'you are your own master; you may go or stay. But I warn you, your friend may prove less powerful than your enemies. The Prince, indeed, is thoroughly on your side; he has all the will to help; but to whom do I speak?—you know better than I do, he is not alone in Grünewald.'

'There is a deal in position,' returned the traveller, gravely nodding. 'Gondremark loves to temporise; his policy is below ground, and he fears all open courses; and now that I have seen you act with so much spirit, I will cheerfully risk myself on your protection. Who knows? You may be yet the better man.'

'Do you indeed believe so?' cried the Prince. 'You put life into my heart!'

'I will give up sketching portraits,' said the Baronet. 'I am a blind owl; I had misread you strangely. And yet remember this; a sprint is one thing, and to run all day another. For I still mistrust your constitution; the short nose, the hair and eyes of several complexions; no, they are diagnostic; and I must end, I see, as I began.'

'I am still a singing chambermaid?' said Otto.

'Nay, your Highness, I pray you to forget what I had written,' said Sir John; 'I am not like Pilate; and the chapter is no more. Bury it, if you love me.'

CHAPTER IV
WHILE THE PRINCE IS IN
THE ANTE-ROOM . . .

Greatly comforted by the exploits of the morning, the Prince turned towards the Princess's ante-room, bent on a more difficult enterprise. The curtains rose before him, the usher called his name, and he entered the room with an exaggeration of his usual mincing and airy dignity. There were about a score of persons waiting, principally ladies; it was one of the few societies in Grünewald where Otto knew himself to be popular; and while a maid of honour made her exit by a side door to announce his arrival to the Princess, he moved round the apartment, collecting homage and bestowing compliments with friendly grace. Had this been the sum of his duties, he had been an admirable monarch. Lady after lady was impartially honoured by his attention.

'Madam,' he said to one, 'how does this happen? I find you daily more adorable.'

'And your Highness daily browner,' replied the lady. 'We began equal; O, there I will be bold: we have both beautiful complexions. But while I study mine, your Highness tans himself.'

'A perfect negro, madam; and what so fitly—being beauty's slave?' said Otto.—'Madame Grafinski, when is our next play? I have just heard that I am a bad actor.'

'*O ciel!*' cried Madame Grafinski. 'Who could venture? What a bear!'

'An excellent man, I can assure you,' returned Otto.

'O, never! O, is it possible!' fluted the lady. 'Your Highness plays like an angel.'

'You must be right, madam; who could speak falsely and yet look so charming?' said the Prince. 'But this gentleman, it seems, would have preferred me playing like an actor.'

A sort of hum, a falsetto, feminine cooing, greeted the tiny sally; and Otto expanded like a peacock. This warm atmosphere of women and flattery and idle chatter pleased him to the marrow.

'Madame von Eisenthal, your coiffure is delicious,' he remarked.

'Every one was saying so,' said one.

'If I have pleased Prince Charming?' And Madame von Eisenthal swept him a deep curtsy with a killing glance of adoration.

'It is new?' he asked. 'Vienna fashion.'

'Mint new,' replied the lady, 'for your Highness's return. I felt young this morning; it was a premonition. But why, Prince, do you ever leave us?'

'For the pleasure of the return,' said Otto. 'I am like a dog; I must bury my bone, and then come back to great upon it.'

'O, a bone! Fie, what a comparison! You have brought back the manners of the wood,' returned the lady.

'Madam, it is what the dog has dearest,' said the Prince. 'But I observe Madame von Rosen.'

And Otto, leaving the group to which he had been piping, stepped towards the embrasure of a window where a lady stood.

The Countess von Rosen had hitherto been silent, and a thought depressed, but on the approach of Otto she began to brighten. She was tall, slim as a nymph, and of a very airy carriage; and her face, which was already beautiful in repose, lightened and changed, flashed into smiles, and glowed with lovely colour at the touch of animation. She was a good vocalist; and, even in speech, her voice commanded a great range of changes, the low notes rich with tenor quality, the upper ringing, on the brink of laughter, into music. A gem of many facets and variable hues of fire; a woman who withheld the better portion of her beauty, and then, in a caressing second, flashed it like a weapon full on the beholder; now merely a tall figure and a sallow handsome face, with the evidences of a reckless temper; anon opening like a flower to life and colour, mirth and tenderness:—Madame von Rosen had always a dagger in reserve for the despatch of ill-assured admirers. She met Otto with the dart of tender gaiety.

'You have come to me at last, Prince Cruel,' she said. 'Butterfly! Well, and am I not to kiss your hand?' she added.

'Madam, it is I who must kiss yours.' And Otto bowed and kissed it.

'You deny me every indulgence,' she said, smiling.

'And now what news in Court?' inquired the Prince. 'I come to you for my gazette.'

'Ditch-water!' she replied. 'The world is all asleep, grown grey in slumber; I do not remember any waking movement since quite an eternity; and the last thing in the nature of a sensation was the last time my governess was allowed to box my ears. But yet I do myself and your unfortunate enchanted palace some injustice. Here is the last—O positively!' And she told him the story from behind her fan, with many glances, many cunning strokes of the narrator's art. The others had drawn away, for it was understood that Madame von Rosen was in favour with the Prince. None the less, however, did the Countess lower her voice at times to within a semitone of whispering; and the pair leaned together over the narrative.

'Do you know,' said Otto, laughing, 'you are the only entertaining woman on this earth!'

'O, you have found out so much,' she cried.

'Yes, madam, I grow wiser with advancing years,' he returned.

'Years,' she repeated. 'Do you name the traitors? I do not believe in years; the calendar is a delusion.'

'You must be right, madam,' replied the Prince. 'For six years that we have been good friends, I have observed you to grow younger.'

'Flatterer!' cried she, and then with a change, 'But why should I say so,' she added, 'when I protest I think the same? A week ago I had a council with my father director, the glass; and the glass replied, "Not yet!" I confess my face in this way once a month. O! a very solemn moment. Do you know what I shall do when the mirror answers, "Now"?'

'I cannot guess,' said he.

'No more can I,' returned the Countess. 'There is such a choice! Suicide, gambling, a nunnery, a volume of memoirs, or politics—the last, I am afraid.'

'It is a dull trade,' said Otto.

'Nay,' she replied, 'it is a trade I rather like. It is, after all, first cousin to gossip, which no one can deny to be amusing. For instance, if I were to tell you that the Princess and the Baron rode out together daily to inspect the cannon, it is either a piece of politics or scandal, as I turn my phrase. I am the alchemist that makes the transmutation. They have been everywhere together since you left,' she continued, brightening as she saw Otto darken; 'that is a poor snippet of malicious gossip—and they were everywhere cheered—and with that addition all becomes political intelligence.'

'Let us change the subject,' said Otto.

'I was about to propose it,' she replied, 'or rather to pursue the politics. Do you know? this war is popular—popular to the length of cheering Princess Seraphina.'

'All things, madam, are possible,' said the Prince; and this among others, that we may be going into war, but I give you my word of honour I do not know with whom.'

'And you put up with it?' she cried. 'I have no pretensions to morality; and I confess I have always abominated the lamb, and nourished a romantic feeling for the wolf. O, be done with lambiness! Let us see there is a prince, for I am weary of the distaff.'

'Madam,' said Otto, 'I thought you were of that faction.'

'I should be of yours, *mon Prince*, if you had one,' she retorted. 'Is it true that you have no ambition? There was a man once in England whom they call the kingmaker. Do you know,' she added, 'I fancy I could make a prince?'

'Some day, madam,' said Otto, 'I may ask you to help make a farmer.'

'Is that a riddle?' asked the Countess.

'It is,' replied the Prince, 'and a very good one too.'

'Tit for tat. I will ask you another,' she returned. 'Where is Gondremark?'

'The Prime Minister? In the prime-ministry, no doubt,' said Otto.

'Precisely,' said the Countess; and she pointed with her fan to the door of the Princess's apartments. 'You and I, *mon Prince*, are in the ante-room. You think me unkind,' she added. 'Try me and you will see. Set me a task, put me a question; there is no enormity I am not capable of doing to oblige you, and no secret that I am not ready to betray.'

'Nay, madam, but I respect my friend too much,' he answered, kissing her hand. 'I would rather remain ignorant of all. We fraternise like foemen soldiers at the outposts, but let each be true to his own army.'

'Ah,' she cried, 'if all men were generous like you, it would be worth while to be a woman!' Yet, judging by her looks, his generosity, if anything, had disappointed her; she seemed to seek a remedy, and, having found it, brightened once more. 'And now,' she said, 'may I dismiss my sovereign? This is rebellion and a *cas pendable*; but what am I to do? My bear is jealous!'

'Madam, enough!' cried Otto. 'Ahasuerus reaches you the sceptre; more, he will obey you in all points. I should have been a dog to come to whistling.'

And so the Prince departed, and fluttered round Grafinski and von Eisenthal. But the Countess knew the use of her offensive weapons, and had left a pleasant arrow in the Prince's heart. That Gondremark was jealous—here was an agreeable revenge! And Madame von Rosen, as the occasion of the jealousy, appeared to him in a new light.

CHAPTER V
... GONDREMARK IS IN MY LADY'S CHAMBER

The Countess von Rosen spoke the truth. The great Prime Minister of Grünewald was already closeted with Seraphina. The toilet was over; and the Princess, tastefully arrayed, sat face to face with a tall mirror. Sir John's description was unkindly true, true in terms and yet a libel, a misogynistic masterpiece. Her forehead was perhaps too high, but it became her; her figure somewhat stooped, but every detail was formed and finished like a gem; her hand, her foot, her ear, the set of her comely head, were all dainty and accordant; if she was not beautiful, she was vivid, changeful, coloured, and pretty with a thousand various prettinesses; and her eyes, if they indeed rolled too consciously, yet rolled to purpose. They were her most attractive feature, yet they continually bore eloquent false witness to her thoughts; for while she herself, in the depths of her immature, unsoftened heart, was given altogether to manlike ambition and the desire of power, the eyes were by turns bold, inviting, fiery, melting, and artful, like the eyes of a rapacious siren. And artful, in a sense, she was. Chafing that she was not a man, and could not shine by action, she had conceived a woman's part, of answerable domination; she sought to subjugate for by-ends, to rain influence and be fancy free; and, while she loved not man, loved to see man obey her. It is a common girl's ambition. Such was perhaps that lady of the glove, who sent her lover to the lions. But the snare is laid alike for male and female, and the world most artfully contrived.

Near her, in a low chair, Gondremark had arranged his limbs into a cat-like attitude, high-shouldered, stooping, and submiss. The formidable blue jowl of the man, and the dull bilious eye, set perhaps a higher value on his evident desire to please. His face was marked by capacity, temper, and a kind of bold, piratical dishonesty which it would be calumnious to call deceit. His manners, as he smiled upon the Princess, were over-fine, yet hardly elegant.

'Possibly,' said the Baron, 'I should now proceed to take my leave. I must not keep my sovereign in the ante-room. Let us come at once to a decision.'

'It cannot, cannot be put off?' she asked.

'It is impossible,' answered Gondremark. 'Your Highness sees it for herself. In the earlier stages, we might imitate the serpent; but for the ultimatum, there is no choice but to be bold like lions. Had the Prince chosen to remain away, it had been better; but we have gone too far forward to delay.'

'What can have brought him?' she cried. 'To-day of all days?'

'The marplot, madam, has the instinct of his nature,' returned Gondremark. 'But you exaggerate the peril. Think, madam, how far we have prospered, and against what odds! Shall a Featherhead?—but no!' And he blew upon his fingers lightly with a laugh.

'Featherhead,' she replied, 'is still the Prince of Grünewald.'

'On your sufferance only, and so long as you shall please to be indulgent,' said the Baron. 'There are rights of nature; power to the powerful is the law. If he shall think to cross your destiny—well, you have heard of the brazen and the earthen pot.'

'Do you call me pot? You are ungallant, Baron,' laughed the Princess.

'Before we are done with your glory, I shall have called you by many different titles,' he replied.

The girl flushed with pleasure. 'But Frédéric is still the Prince, *monsieur le flatteur*,' she said. 'You do not propose a revolution?—you of all men?'

'Dear madam, when it is already made!' he cried. 'The Prince reigns indeed in the almanac; but my Princess reigns and rules.' And he looked at her with a fond admiration that made the heart of Seraphina swell. Looking on her huge slave, she drank the intoxicating joys of power. Meanwhile he continued, with that sort of massive archness that so ill became him, 'She has but one fault; there is but one danger in the great career that I foresee for her. May I name it? may I be so irreverent? It is in herself—her heart is soft.'

'Her courage is faint, Baron,' said the Princess. 'Suppose we have judged ill, suppose we were defeated?'

'Defeated, madam?' returned the Baron, with a touch of ill-humour. 'Is the dog defeated by the hare? Our troops are all cantoned along the frontier; in five hours the vanguard of five thousand bayonets shall be hammering on the gates of Brandenau; and in all Gerolstein there are not fifteen hundred men who can manœuvre. It is as simple as a sum. There can be no resistance.'

'It is no great exploit,' she said. 'Is that what you call glory? It is like beating a child.'

'The courage, madam, is diplomatic,' he replied. 'We take a grave step; we fix the eyes of Europe, for the first time, on Grünewald; and in the negotiations of the next three months, mark me, we stand or fall. It is there, madam, that I shall have to depend upon your counsels,' he added, almost gloomily. 'If I had not seen you at work, if I did not know the fertility of your mind, I own I should tremble for the consequence. But it is in this field that men must recognise their inability. All the great negotiators, when they have not been women, have had women at their elbows. Madame de Pompadour was ill served; she had not found her Gondremark; but what a mighty politician! Catherine de' Medici, too, what justice of sight, what readiness of means, what elasticity against defeat! But alas! madam, her Featherheads were her own children; and she had that one touch of vulgarity, that one trait of the good-wife, that she suffered family ties and affections to confine her liberty.'

These singular views of history, strictly *ad usum Seraphinæ*, did not weave their usual soothing spell over the Princess. It was plain that she had taken a momentary distaste to her own resolutions; for she continued to oppose her counsellor, looking upon him out of half-closed eyes and with the shadow of a sneer upon her lips. 'What boys men are!' she said; 'what lovers of big words! Courage, indeed! If you had to scour pans, Herr Von Gondremark, you would call it, I suppose, Domestic Courage?'

'I would, madam,' said the Baron stoutly, 'if I scoured them well. I would put a good name upon a virtue; you will not overdo it: they are not so enchanting in themselves.'

'Well, but let me see,' she said. 'I wish to understand your courage. Why we asked leave, like children! Our grannie in Berlin, our uncle in Vienna, the whole family, have patted us on the head and sent us forward. Courage? I wonder when I hear you!'

'My Princess is unlike herself,' returned the Baron. 'She has forgotten where the peril lies. True, we have received encouragement on every hand; but my Princess knows too well on what untenable conditions; and she knows besides how, in the publicity of the diet, these whispered conferences are forgotten and disowned. The danger is very real'—he raged inwardly at having to blow the very coal he had been quenching—'none the less real in that it is not precisely military, but for that reason the easier to be faced. Had we to count upon your troops, although I share your Highness's expectations of the conduct of Alvenau, we cannot forget that he has not been proved in chief command. But where negotiation is concerned, the conduct lies with us; and with your help, I laugh at danger.'

'It may be so,' said Seraphina, sighing. 'It is elsewhere that I see danger. The people, these abominable people—suppose they should instantly rebel? What a figure we should make in the eyes of Europe to have undertaken an invasion while my own throne was tottering to its fall!'

'Nay, madam,' said Gondremark, smiling, 'here you are beneath yourself. What is it that feeds their discontent? What but the taxes? Once we have seized Gerolstein, the taxes are remitted, the sons return covered with renown, the houses are adorned with pillage, each tastes his little share of military glory, and behold us once again a happy family! "Ay," they will say, in each other's long ears, "the Princess knew what she was about; she was in the right of it; she has a head upon her shoulders; and here we are, you see, better off than before." But why should I say all this? It is what my Princess pointed out to me herself; it was by these reasons that she converted me to this adventure.'

'I think, Herr von Gondremark,' said Seraphina, somewhat tartly, 'you often attribute your own sagacity to your Princess.'

For a second Gondremark staggered under the shrewdness of the attack; the next, he had perfectly recovered. 'Do I?' he said. 'It is very possible. I have observed a similar tendency in your Highness.'

It was so openly spoken, and appeared so just, that Seraphina breathed again. Her vanity had been alarmed, and the greatness of the relief improved her spirits. 'Well,' she said, 'all this is little to the purpose. We are keeping Frédéric without, and I am still ignorant of our line of battle. Come, co-admiral, let us consult. . . . How am I to receive him now? And what are we to do if he should appear at the council?'

'Now,' he answered. 'I shall leave him to my Princess for just now! I have seen her at work. Send him off to his theatricals! But in all gentleness,' he added. 'Would it, for instance, would it displease my sovereign to affect a headache?'

'Never!' said she. 'The woman who can manage, like the man who can fight, must never shrink from an encounter. The knight must not disgrace his weapons.'

'Then let me pray my *belle dame sans merci*,' he returned, 'to affect the only virtue that she lacks. Be pitiful to the poor young man; affect an interest in his hunting; be weary of politics; find in his society, as it were, a grateful repose from dry considerations. Does my Princess authorise the line of battle?'

'Well, that is a trifle,' answered Seraphina. 'The council—there is the point.'

'The council?' cried Gondremark. 'Permit me, madam.' And he rose and proceeded to flutter about the room, counterfeiting Otto both in voice and gesture not unhappily. 'What is there to-day, Herr von Gondremark? Ah, Herr Cancellarius, a new wig! You cannot deceive me; I know every wig in Grünewald; I have the sovereign's eye. What are these papers about? O, I see. O, certainly. Surely, surely. I wager none of you remarked that wig. By all means. I know nothing about that. Dear me, are there as many as all that? Well, you can sign them; you have the procuration. You see, Herr Cancellarius, I knew your wig. And so,' concluded Gondremark, resuming his own voice, 'our sovereign, by the particular grace of God, enlightens and supports his privy councillors.'

But when the Baron turned to Seraphina for approval, he found her frozen. 'You are pleased to be witty, Herr von Gondremark,' she said, 'and have perhaps forgotten where you are. But these rehearsals are apt to be misleading. Your master, the Prince of Grünewald, is sometimes more exacting.'

Gondremark cursed her in his soul. Of all injured vanities, that of the reproved buffoon is the most savage; and when grave issues are involved, these petty stabs become unbearable. But Gondremark was a man of iron; he showed nothing; he did not even, like the common trickster, retreat because he had presumed, but held to his point bravely. 'Madam,' he said, 'if, as you say, he prove exacting, we must take the bull by the horns.'

'We shall see,' she said, and she arranged her skirt like one about to rise. Temper, scorn, disgust, all the more acrid feelings, became her like jewels; and she now looked her best.

'Pray God they quarrel,' thought Gondremark. 'The damned minx may fail me yet, unless they quarrel. It is time to let him in. Zz—fight, dogs!' Consequent on these reflections, he bent a stiff knee and chivalrously kissed the Princess's hand. 'My Princess,' he said, 'must now dismiss her servant. I have much to arrange against the hour of council.'

'Go,' she said, and rose.

And as Gondremark tripped out of a private door, she touched a bell, and gave the order to admit the Prince.

CHAPTER VI
THE PRINCE DELIVERS A LECTURE ON MARRIAGE, WITH PRACTICAL ILLUSTRATIONS OF DIVORCE

With what a world of excellent intentions Otto entered his wife's cabinet! how fatherly, how tender! how morally affecting were the words he had prepared! Nor was Seraphina unamiably inclined. Her usual fear of Otto as a marplot in her great designs was now swallowed up in a passing distrust of the designs themselves. For Gondremark, besides, she had conceived an angry horror. In her heart she did not like the Baron. Behind his impudent servility, behind the devotion which, with indelicate delicacy, he still forced on her attention, she divined the grossness of his nature. So a man may be proud of having tamed a bear, and yet sicken at his captive's odour. And above all, she had certain jealous intimations that the man was false and the deception double. True, she falsely trifled with his love; but he, perhaps, was only trifling with her vanity. The insolence of his late mimicry, and the odium of her own position as she sat and watched it, lay besides like a load upon her conscience. She met Otto almost with a sense of guilt, and yet she welcomed him as a deliverer from ugly things.

But the wheels of an interview are at the mercy of a thousand ruts; and even at Otto's entrance, the first jolt occurred. Gondremark, he saw, was gone; but there was the chair drawn close for consultation; and it pained him not only that this man had been received, but that he should depart with such an air of secrecy. Struggling with this twinge, it was somewhat sharply that he dismissed the attendant who had brought him in.

'You make yourself at home, *chez moi*,' she said, a little ruffled both by his tone of command and by the glance he had thrown upon the chair.

'Madam,' replied Otto, 'I am here so seldom that I have almost the rights of a stranger.'

'You choose your own associates, Frédéric,' she said.

'I am here to speak of it,' he returned. 'It is now four years since we were married; and these four years, Seraphina, have not perhaps been happy either for you or for me. I am well aware I was unsuitable to be your husband. I was not young, I had no ambition, I was a trifler; and you despised me, I dare not say unjustly. But to do justice on both sides, you must bear in mind how I have acted. When I found it amused you to play the part of Princess on this little stage, did I not immediately resign to you my box of toys, this Grünewald? And when I found I was distasteful as a husband, could any husband have been less intrusive? You will tell me that I have no feelings, no preference, and thus no credit; that I go before the wind; that all this was in my character. And indeed, one thing is true, that it is easy, too easy, to leave things undone. But Seraphina, I begin to learn it is not always wise. If I were too old and too uncongenial for your husband, I should still have remembered that I was the Prince of that country to which you came, a visitor and a child. In that relation also there were duties, and these duties I have not performed.'

To claim the advantage of superior age is to give sure offence. 'Duty!' laughed Seraphina, 'and on your lips, Frédéric! You make me laugh. What fancy is this? Go, flirt with the maids and be a prince in Dresden china, as you look. Enjoy yourself, *mon enfant*, and leave duty and the state to us.'

The plural grated on the Prince. 'I have enjoyed myself too much,' he said, 'since enjoyment is the word. And yet there were much to say upon the other side. You must suppose me desperately fond of hunting. But indeed there were days when I found a great deal of interest in what it was courtesy to call my government. And I have always had some claim to taste; I could tell live happiness from dull routine; and between hunting, and the throne of Austria, and your society, my choice had never wavered, had the choice been mine. You were a girl, a bud, when you were given me—'

'Heavens!' she cried, 'is this to be a love-scene?'

'I am never ridiculous,' he said; 'it is my only merit; and you may be certain this shall be a scene of marriage *à la mode*. But when I remember the beginning, it is bare courtesy to speak in sorrow. Be just, madam: you would think me strangely uncivil to recall these days without the decency of a regret. Be yet a little juster, and own, if only in complaisance, that you yourself regret that past.'

'I have nothing to regret,' said the Princess. 'You surprise me. I thought you were so happy.'

'Happy and happy, there are so many hundred ways,' said Otto. 'A man may be happy in revolt; he may be happy in sleep; wine, change, and travel make him happy; virtue, they say, will do the like—I have not tried; and they say also that in old, quiet, and habitual marriages there is yet another happiness. Happy, yes; I am happy if you like; but I will tell you frankly, I was happier when I brought you home.'

'Well,' said the Princess, not without constraint, 'it seems you changed your mind.'

'Not I,' returned Otto, 'I never changed. Do you remember, Seraphina, on our way home, when you saw the roses in the lane, and I got out and plucked them? It was a narrow lane between great trees; the sunset at the end was all gold, and the rooks were flying overhead. There were nine, nine red roses; you gave me a kiss for each, and I told myself that every rose and every kiss should stand for a year of love. Well, in eighteen months there was an end. But do you fancy, Seraphina, that my heart has altered?'

'I am sure I cannot tell,' she said, like an automaton.

'It has not,' the Prince continued. 'There is nothing ridiculous, even from a husband, in a love that owns itself unhappy and that asks no more. I built on sand; pardon me, I do not breathe a reproach—I built, I suppose, upon my own infirmities; but I put my heart in the building, and it still lies among the ruins.'

'How very poetical!' she said, with a little choking laugh, unknown relentings, unfamiliar softnesses, moving within her. 'What would you be at?' she added, hardening her voice.

'I would be at this,' he answered; 'and hard it is to say. I would be at this:—Seraphina, I am your husband after all, and a poor fool that loves you. Understand,' he cried almost fiercely, 'I am no suppliant husband; what your love refuses I would scorn to receive from your pity. I do not ask, I would not take it. And for jealousy, what ground have I? A dog-in-the-manger jealousy is a thing the dogs may laugh at. But at least, in the world's eye, I am still your husband; and I ask you if you treat me fairly? I keep to myself, I leave you free, I have given you in everything your will. What do you in return? I find, Seraphina, that you have been too thoughtless. But between persons such as we are, in our conspicuous station, particular care and a particular courtesy are owing. Scandal is perhaps not easy to avoid; but it is hard to bear.'

'Scandal!' she cried, with a deep breath. 'Scandal! It is for this you have been driving!'

'I have tried to tell you how I feel,' he replied. 'I have told you that I love you—love you in vain—a bitter thing for a husband; I have laid myself open that I might speak without offence. And now that I have begun, I will go on and finish.'

'I demand it,' she said. 'What is this about?'

Otto flushed crimson. 'I have to say what I would fain not,' he answered. 'I counsel you to see less of Gondremark.'

'Of Gondremark? And why?' she asked.

'Your intimacy is the ground of scandal, madam,' said Otto, firmly enough—'of a scandal that is agony to me, and would be crushing to your parents if they knew it.'

'You are the first to bring me word of it,' said she. 'I thank you.'

'You have perhaps cause,' he replied. 'Perhaps I am the only one among your friends—'

'O, leave my friends alone,' she interrupted. 'My friends are of a different stamp. You have come to me here and made a parade of sentiment. When have I last seen you? I have governed your kingdom for you in the meanwhile, and there I got no help. At last, when I am weary with a man's work, and you are weary of your playthings, you return to make me a scene of conjugal reproaches—the grocer and his wife! The positions are too much reversed; and you should understand, at least, that I cannot at the same time do your work of government and behave myself like a little girl. Scandal is the atmosphere in which we live, we princes; it is what a prince should know. You play an odious part. Do you believe this rumour?'

'Madam, should I be here?' said Otto.

'It is what I want to know!' she cried, the tempest of her scorn increasing. 'Suppose you did—I say, suppose you did believe it?'

'I should make it my business to suppose the contrary,' he answered.

'I thought so. O, you are made of baseness!' said she.

'Madam,' he cried, roused at last, 'enough of this. You wilfully misunderstand my attitude; you outwear my patience. In the name of your parents, in my own name, I summon you to be more circumspect.'

'Is this a request, *monsieur mon mari?*' she demanded.

'Madam, if I chose, I might command,' said Otto.

'You might, sir, as the law stands, make me prisoner,' returned Seraphina. 'Short of that you will gain nothing.'

'You will continue as before?' he asked.

'Precisely as before,' said she. 'As soon as this comedy is over, I shall request the Freiherr von Gondremark to visit me. Do you understand?' she added, rising. 'For my part, I have done.'

'I will then ask the favour of your hand, madam,' said Otto, palpitating in every pulse with anger. 'I have to request that you will visit in my society another part of my poor house. And reassure yourself—it will not take long—and it is the last obligation that you shall have the chance to lay me under.'

'The last?' she cried. 'Most joyfully?'

She offered her hand, and he took it; on each side with an elaborate affectation, each inwardly incandescent. He led her out by the private door, following where Gondremark had passed; they threaded a corridor or two, little frequented, looking on a court, until they came at last into the Prince's suite. The first room was an armoury, hung all about with the weapons of various countries, and looking forth on the front terrace.

'Have you brought me here to slay me?' she inquired.

'I have brought you, madam, only to pass on,' replied Otto.

Next they came to a library, where an old chamberlain sat half asleep. He rose and bowed before the princely couple, asking for orders.

'You will attend us here,' said Otto.

The next stage was a gallery of pictures, where Seraphina's portrait hung conspicuous, dressed for the chase, red roses in her hair, as Otto, in the first months of marriage, had directed. He pointed to it without a word; she raised her eyebrows in silence; and they passed still forward into a matted corridor where four doors opened. One led to Otto's bedroom; one was the private door to Seraphina's. And here, for the first time, Otto left her hand, and stepping forward, shot the bolt.

'It is long, madam,' said he, 'since it was bolted on the other side.'

'One was effectual,' returned the Princess. 'Is this all?'

'Shall I reconduct you?' he asking, bowing.

'I should prefer,' she asked, in ringing tones, 'the conduct of the Freiherr von Gondremark.'

Otto summoned the chamberlain. 'If the Freiherr von Gondremark is in the palace,' he said, 'bid him attend the Princess here.' And when the official had departed, 'Can I do more to serve you, madam?' the Prince asked.

'Thank you, no. I have been much amused,' she answered.

'I have now,' continued Otto, 'given you your liberty complete. This has been for you a miserable marriage.'

'Miserable!' said she.

'It has been made light to you; it shall be lighter still,' continued the Prince. 'But one thing, madam, you must still continue to bear—my father's name, which is now yours. I leave it in your hands. Let me see you, since you will have no advice of mine, apply the more attention of your own to bear it worthily.'

'Herr von Gondremark is long in coming,' she remarked.

'O Seraphina, Seraphina!' he cried. And that was the end of their interview.

She tripped to a window and looked out; and a little after, the chamberlain announced the Freiherr von Gondremark, who entered with something of a wild eye and changed complexion, confounded, as he was, at this unusual summons. The Princess faced round from the window with a pearly smile; nothing but her heightened colour spoke of discomposure.

Otto was pale, but he was otherwise master of himself.

'Herr von Gondremark,' said he, 'oblige me so far: reconduct the Princess to her own apartment.'

The Baron, still all at sea, offered his hand, which was smilingly accepted, and the pair sailed forth through the picture-gallery.

As soon as they were gone, and Otto knew the length and breadth of his miscarriage, and how he had done the contrary of all that he intended, he stood stupefied. A fiasco so complete and sweeping was laughable, even to himself; and he laughed aloud in his wrath. Upon this mood there followed the sharpest violence of remorse; and to that again, as he recalled his provocation, anger succeeded afresh. So he was tossed in spirit; now bewailing his inconsequence and lack of temper, now flaming up in white-hot indignation and a noble pity for himself.

He paced his apartment like a leopard. There was danger in Otto, for a flash. Like a pistol, he could kill at one moment, and the next he might he kicked aside. But just then, as he walked the long floors in his alternate humours, tearing his handkerchief between his hands, he was strung to his top note, every nerve attent. The pistol, you might say, was charged. And when jealousy from time to time fetched him a lash across the tenderest of his feeling, and sent a string of her fire-pictures glancing before his mind's eye, the contraction of his face was even dangerous. He disregarded jealousy's inventions, yet they stung. In this height of anger, he still preserved his faith in Seraphina's innocence; but the thought of her possible misconduct was the bitterest ingredient in his pot of sorrow.

There came a knock at the door, and the chamberlain brought him a note. He took it and ground it in his hand, continuing his march, continuing his bewildered thoughts; and some minutes had gone by before the circumstance came clearly to his mind. Then he paused and opened it. It was a pencil scratch from Gotthold, thus conceived:

'The council is privately summoned at once.

G. v. H.'

If the council was thus called before the hour, and that privately, it was plain they feared his interference. Feared: here was a sweet thought. Gotthold, too—Gotthold, who had always used and regarded him as a mere peasant lad, had now been at the pains to warn him; Gotthold looked for something at his hands. Well, none should be disappointed; the Prince, too long beshadowed by the uxorious lover, should now return and shine. He summoned his valet, repaired the disorder of his appearance with elaborate care; and then, curled and scented and adorned, Prince Charming in every line, but with a twitching nostril, he set forth unattended for the council.

CHAPTER VII
THE PRINCE DISSOLVES THE COUNCIL

It was as Gotthold wrote. The liberation of Sir John, Greisengesang's uneasy narrative, last of all, the scene between Seraphina and the Prince, had decided the conspirators to take a step of bold timidity. There had been a period of bustle, liveried messengers speeding here and there with notes; and at half-past ten in the morning, about an hour before its usual hour, the council of Grünewald sat around the board.

It was not a large body. At the instance of Gondremark, it had undergone a strict purgation, and was now composed exclusively of tools. Three secretaries sat at a side-table. Seraphina took the head; on her right was the Baron, on her left Greisengesang; below these Grafinski the treasurer, Count Eisenthal, a couple of non-combatants, and, to the surprise of all, Gotthold. He had been named a privy councillor by Otto, merely that he might profit by the salary; and as he was never known to attend a meeting, it had occurred to nobody to cancel his appointment. His present appearance was the more ominous, coming when it did. Gondremark scowled upon him; and the non-combatant on his right, intercepting this black look, edged away from one who was so clearly out of favour.

'The hour presses, your Highness,' said the Baron; 'may we proceed to business?'

'At once,' replied Seraphina.

'Your Highness will pardon me,' said Gotthold; 'but you are still, perhaps, unacquainted with the fact that Prince Otto has returned.'

'The Prince will not attend the council,' replied Seraphina, with a momentary blush. 'The despatches, Herr Cancellarius? There is one for Gerolstein?'

A secretary brought a paper.

'Here, madam,' said Greisengesang. 'Shall I read it?'

'We are all familiar with its terms,' replied Gondremark. 'Your Highness approves?'

'Unhesitatingly,' said Seraphina.

'It may then be held as read,' concluded the Baron. 'Will your Highness sign?'

The Princess did so; Gondremark, Eisenthal, and one of the non-combatants followed suit; and the paper was then passed across the table to the librarian. He proceeded leisurely to read.

'We have no time to spare, Herr Doctor,' cried the Baron brutally. 'If you do not choose to sign on the authority of your sovereign, pass it on. Or you may leave the table,' he added, his temper ripping out.

'I decline your invitation, Herr von Gondremark; and my sovereign, as I continue to observe with regret, is still absent from the board,' replied the Doctor calmly; and he resumed the perusal of the paper, the rest chafing and exchanging glances. 'Madame and gentlemen,' he said, at last, 'what I hold in my hand is simply a declaration of war.'

'Simply,' said Seraphina, flashing defiance.

'The sovereign of this country is under the same roof with us,' continued Gotthold, 'and I insist he shall be summoned. It is needless to adduce my reasons; you are all ashamed at heart of this projected treachery.'

The council waved like a sea. There were various outcries.

'You insult the Princess,' thundered Gondremark.

'I maintain my protest,' replied Gotthold.

At the height of this confusion the door was thrown open; an usher announced, 'Gentlemen, the Prince!' and Otto, with his most excellent bearing, entered the apartment. It was like oil upon the troubled waters; every one settled instantly into his place, and Griesengesang, to give himself a countenance, became absorbed in the arrangement of his papers; but in their eagerness to dissemble, one and all neglected to rise.

'Gentlemen,' said the Prince, pausing.

They all got to their feet in a moment; and this reproof still further demoralised the weaker brethren.

The Prince moved slowly towards the lower end of the table; then he paused again, and, fixing his eye on Greisengesang, 'How comes it, Herr Cancellarius,' he asked, 'that I have received no notice of the change of hour?'

'Your Highness,' replied the Chancellor, 'her Highness the Princess . . . ' and there paused.

'I understood,' said Seraphina, taking him up, 'that you did not purpose to be present.'

Their eyes met for a second, and Seraphina's fell; but her anger only burned the brighter for that private shame.

'And now, gentlemen,' said Otto, taking his chair, 'I pray you to be seated. I have been absent: there are doubtless some arrears; but ere we proceed to business, Herr Grafinski, you will direct four thousand crowns to be sent to me at once. Make a note, if you please,' he added, as the treasurer still stared in wonder.

'Four thousand crowns?' asked Seraphina. 'Pray, for what?'

'Madam,' returned Otto, smiling, 'for my own purposes.'

Gondremark spurred up Grafinski underneath the table.

'If your Highness will indicate the destination . . . ' began the puppet.

'You are not here, sir, to interrogate your Prince,' said Otto.

Grafinski looked for help to his commander; and Gondremark came to his aid, in suave and measured tones.

'Your Highness may reasonably be surprised,' he said; 'and Herr Grafinski, although I am convinced he is clear of the intention of offending, would have perhaps done better to begin with an explanation. The resources of the state are at the present moment entirely swallowed up, or, as we hope to prove, wisely invested. In a month from now, I do not question we shall be able to meet any command your Highness may lay upon us; but at this hour I fear that, even in so small a matter, he must prepare himself for disappointment. Our zeal is no less, although our power may be inadequate.'

'How much, Herr Grafinski, have we in the treasury?' asked Otto.

'Your Highness,' protested the treasurer, 'we have immediate need of every crown.'

'I think, sir, you evade me,' flashed the Prince; and then turning to the side-table, 'Mr. Secretary,' he added, 'bring me, if you please, the treasury docket.'

Herr Grafinski became deadly pale; the Chancellor, expecting his own turn, was probably engaged in prayer; Gondremark was watching like a ponderous cat. Gotthold, on his part, looked on with wonder at his cousin; he was certainly showing spirit, but what, in such a time of gravity, was all this talk of money? and why should he waste his strength upon a personal issue?

'I find,' said Otto, with his finger on the docket, 'that we have 20,000 crowns in case.'

'That is exact, your Highness,' replied the Baron. 'But our liabilities, all of which are happily not liquid, amount to a far larger sum; and at the present point of time it would be morally impossible to divert a single florin. Essentially, the case is empty. We have, already presented, a large note for material of war.'

'Material of war?' exclaimed Otto, with an excellent assumption of surprise. 'But if my memory serves me right, we settled these accounts in January.'

'There have been further orders,' the Baron explained. 'A new park of artillery has been completed; five hundred stand of arms, seven hundred baggage mules—the details are in a special memorandum.—Mr. Secretary Holtz, the memorandum, if you please.'

'One would think, gentlemen, that we were going to war,' said Otto.

'We are,' said Seraphina.

'War!' cried the Prince, 'and, gentlemen, with whom? The peace of Grünewald has endured for centuries. What aggression, what insult, have we suffered?'

'Here, your Highness,' said Gotthold, 'is the ultimatum. It was in the very article of signature, when your Highness so opportunely entered.'

Otto laid the paper before him; as he read, his fingers played tattoo upon the table. 'Was it proposed,' he inquired, 'to send this paper forth without a knowledge of my pleasure?'

One of the non-combatants, eager to trim, volunteered an answer. 'The Herr Doctor von Hohenstockwitz had just entered his dissent,' he added.

'Give me the rest of this correspondence,' said the Prince. It was handed to him, and he read it patiently from end to end, while the councillors sat foolishly enough looking before them on the table.

The secretaries, in the background, were exchanging glances of delight; a row at the council was for them a rare and welcome feature.

'Gentlemen,' said Otto, when he had finished, 'I have read with pain. This claim upon Obermünsterol is palpably unjust; it has not a tincture, not a show, of justice. There is not in all this ground enough for after-dinner talk, and you propose to force it as a *casus belli*.'

'Certainly, your Highness,' returned Gondremark, too wise to defend the indefensible, 'the claim on Obermünsterol is simply a pretext.'

'It is well,' said the Prince. 'Herr Cancellarius, take your pen. "The council," he began to dictate—'I withhold all notice of my intervention,' he said, in parenthesis, and addressing himself more directly to his wife; 'and I say nothing of the strange suppression by which this business has been smuggled past my knowledge. I am content to be in time—"The council,"' he resumed, "'on a further examination of the facts, and enlightened by the note in the last despatch from Gerolstein, have the pleasure to announce that they are entirely at one, both as to fact and sentiment, with the Grand-Ducal Court of Gerolstein." You have it? Upon these lines, sir, you will draw up the despatch.'

'If your Highness will allow me,' said the Baron, 'your Highness is so imperfectly acquainted with the internal history of this correspondence, that any interference will be merely hurtful. Such a paper as your Highness proposes would be to stultify the whole previous policy of Grünewald.'

'The policy of Grünewald!' cried the Prince. 'One would suppose you had no sense of humour! Would you fish in a coffee cup?'

'With deference, your Highness,' returned the Baron, 'even in a coffee cup there may be poison. The purpose of this war is not simply territorial enlargement; still less is it a war of glory; for, as your Highness indicates, the state of Grünewald is too small to be ambitious. But the body politic is seriously diseased; republicanism, socialism, many disintegrating ideas are abroad; circle within circle, a really formidable organisation has grown up about your Highness's throne.'

'I have heard of it, Herr von Gondremark,' put in the Prince; 'but I have reason to be aware that yours is the more authoritative information.'

'I am honoured by this expression of my Prince's confidence' returned Gondremark, unabashed. 'It is, therefore, with a single eye to these disorders that our present external policy has been shaped. Something was required to divert public attention, to employ the idle, to popularise your Highness's rule, and, if it were possible, to enable him to reduce the taxes at a blow and to a notable amount. The proposed expedition—for it cannot without hyperbole be called a war—seemed to the council to combine the various characters required; a marked improvement in the public sentiment has followed even upon our preparations; and I cannot doubt that when success shall follow, the effect will surpass even our boldest hopes.'

'You are very adroit, Herr von Gondremark,' said Otto. 'You fill me with admiration. I had not heretofore done justice to your qualities.'

Seraphina looked up with joy, supposing Otto conquered; but Gondremark still waited, armed at every point; he knew how very stubborn is the revolt of a weak character.

'And the territorial army scheme, to which I was persuaded to consent—was it secretly directed to the same end?' the Prince asked.

'I still believe the effect to have been good,' replied the Baron; 'discipline and mounting guard are excellent sedatives. But I will avow to your Highness, I was unaware, at the date of that decree, of the magnitude of the revolutionary movement; nor did any of us, I think, imagine that such a territorial army was a part of the republican proposals.'

'It was?' asked Otto. 'Strange! Upon what fancied grounds?'

'The grounds were indeed fanciful,' returned the Baron. 'It was conceived among the leaders that a territorial army, drawn from and returning to the people, would, in the event of any popular uprising, prove lukewarm or unfaithful to the throne.'

'I see,' said the Prince. 'I begin to understand.'

'His Highness begins to understand?' repeated Gondremark, with the sweetest politeness. 'May I beg of him to complete the phrase?'

'The history of the revolution,' replied Otto dryly. 'And now,' he added, 'what do you conclude?'

'I conclude, your Highness, with a simple reflection,' said the Baron, accepting the stab without a quiver, 'the war is popular; were the rumour contradicted to-morrow, a considerable disappointment would be felt in many classes; and in the present tension of spirits, the most lukewarm sentiment may be enough to precipitate events. There lies the danger. The revolution hangs imminent; we sit, at this council board, below the sword of Damocles.'

'We must then lay our heads together,' said the Prince, 'and devise some honourable means of safety.'

Up to this moment, since the first note of opposition fell from the librarian, Seraphina had uttered about twenty words. With a somewhat heightened colour, her eyes generally lowered, her foot sometimes nervously tapping on the floor, she had kept her own counsel and commanded her anger like a hero. But at this stage of the engagement she lost control of her impatience.

'Means!' she cried. 'They have been found and prepared before you knew the need for them. Sign the despatch, and let us be done with this delay.'

'Madam, I said "honourable,"' returned Otto, bowing. 'This war is, in my eyes, and by Herr von Gondremark's account, an inadmissible expedient. If we have misgoverned here in Grünewald, are the people of Gerolstein to bleed and pay for our mis-doings? Never, madam; not while I live. But I attach so much importance to all that I have heard to-day for the first time—and why only to-day, I do not even stop to ask—that I am eager to find some plan that I can follow with credit to myself.'

'And should you fail?' she asked.

'Should I fail, I will then meet the blow half-way,' replied the Prince. 'On the first open discontent, I shall convoke the States, and, when it pleases them to bid me, abdicate.'

Seraphina laughed angrily. 'This is the man for whom we have been labouring!' she cried. 'We tell him of change; he will devise the means, he says; and his device is abdication? Sir, have you no shame to come here at the eleventh hour among those who have borne the heat and burthen of the day? Do you not wonder at yourself? I, sir, was here in my place, striving to uphold your dignity alone. I took counsel with the wisest I could find, while you were eating and hunting. I have laid my plans with foresight; they were ripe for action; and then—'she choked—'then you return—for a forenoon—to ruin all! To-morrow, you will be once more about your pleasures; you will give us leave once more to think and work for you; and again you will come back, and again you will thwart what you had not the industry or knowledge to conceive. O! it is intolerable. Be modest, sir. Do not presume upon the rank you cannot worthily uphold. I would not issue my commands with so much gusto—it is from no merit in yourself they are obeyed. What are you? What have you to do in this grave council? Go,' she cried, 'go among your equals? The very people in the streets mock at you for a prince.'

At this surprising outburst the whole council sat aghast.

'Madam,' said the Baron, alarmed out of his caution, 'command yourself.'

'Address yourself to me, sir!' cried the Prince. 'I will not bear these whisperings!'

Seraphina burst into tears.

'Sir,' cried the Baron, rising, 'this lady—'

'Herr von Gondremark,' said the Prince, 'one more observation, and I place you under arrest.'

'Your Highness is the master,' replied Gondremark, bowing.

'Bear it in mind more constantly,' said Otto. 'Herr Cancellarius, bring all the papers to my cabinet. Gentlemen, the council is dissolved.'

And he bowed and left the apartment, followed by Greisengesang and the secretaries, just at the moment when the Princess's ladies, summoned in all haste, entered by another door to help her forth.

CHAPTER VIII
THE PARTY OF WAR TAKES ACTION

Half an hour after, Gondremark was once more closeted with Seraphina.

'Where is he now?' she asked, on his arrival.

'Madam, he is with the Chancellor,' replied the Baron. 'Wonder of wonders, he is at work!'

'Ah,' she said, 'he was born to torture me! O what a fall, what a humiliation! Such a scheme to wreck upon so small a trifle! But now all is lost.'

'Madam,' said Gondremark, 'nothing is lost. Something, on the other hand, is found. You have found your senses; you see him as he is—see him as you see everything where your too-good heart is not in question—with the judicial, with the statesman's eye. So long as he had a right to interfere, the empire that may be was still distant. I have not entered on this course without the plain foresight of its dangers; and even for this I was prepared. But, madam, I knew two things: I knew that you were born to command, that I was born to serve; I knew that by a rare conjuncture, the hand had found the tool; and from the first I was confident, as I am confident to-day, that no hereditary trifler has the power to shatter that alliance.'

'I, born to command!' she said. 'Do you forget my tears?'

'Madam, they were the tears of Alexander,' cried the Baron. 'They touched, they thrilled me; I, forgot myself a moment—even I! But do you suppose that I had not remarked, that I had not admired, your previous bearing? your great self-command? Ay, that was princely!' He paused. 'It was a thing to see. I drank confidence! I tried to imitate your calm. And I was well inspired; in my heart, I think that I was well inspired; that any man, within the reach of argument, had been convinced! But it was not to be; nor, madam, do I regret the failure. Let us be open; let me disclose my heart. I have loved two things, not unworthily: Grünewald and my sovereign!' Here he kissed her hand. 'Either I must resign my ministry, leave the land of my adoption and the queen whom I had chosen to obey— or—' He paused again.

'Alas, Herr von Gondremark, there is no "or,"' said Seraphina.

'Nay, madam, give me time,' he replied. 'When first I saw you, you were still young; not every man would have remarked your powers; but I had not been twice honoured by your conversation ere I had found my mistress. I have, madam, I believe, some genius; and I have much ambition. But the genius is of the serving kind; and to offer a career to my ambition, I had to find one born to rule. This is the base and essence of our union; each had need of the other; each recognised, master and servant, lever and fulcrum, the complement of his endowment. Marriages, they say, are made in heaven: how much more these pure, laborious, intellectual fellowships, born to found empires! Nor is this all. We found each other ripe, filled with great ideas that took shape and clarified with every word. We grew together—ay, madam, in mind we grew together like twin children. All of my life until we met was petty and groping; was it not—I will flatter myself openly—it *was* the same with you! Not till then had you those eagle surveys, that wide and hopeful sweep of intuition! Thus we had formed ourselves, and we were ready.'

'It is true,' she cried. 'I feel it. Yours is the genius; your generosity confounds your insight; all I could offer you was the position, was this throne, to be a fulcrum. But I offered it without reserve; I entered at least warmly into all your thoughts; you were sure of me—sure of my support— certain of justice. Tell me, tell me again, that I have helped you.'

'Nay, madam,' he said, 'you made me. In everything you were my inspiration. And as we prepared our policy, weighing every step, how often have I had to admire your perspicacity, your man-like diligence and fortitude! You know that these are not the words of flattery; your conscience echoes them; have you spared a day? have you indulged yourself in any pleasure? Young and beautiful, you have lived a life of high intellectual effort, of irksome intellectual patience with details. Well, you have your reward: with the fall of Brandenau, the throne of your Empire is founded.'

'What thought have you in your mind?' she asked. 'Is not all ruined?'

'Nay, my Princess, the same thought is in both our minds,' he said.

'Herr von Gondremark,' she replied, 'by all that I hold sacred, I have none; I do not think at all; I am crushed.'

'You are looking at the passionate side of a rich nature, misunderstood and recently insulted,' said the Baron. 'Look into your intellect, and tell me.'

'I find nothing, nothing but tumult,' she replied.

'You find one word branded, madam,' returned the Baron: '"Abdication!"'

'O!' she cried. 'The coward! He leaves me to bear all, and in the hour of trial he stabs me from behind. There is nothing in him, not respect, not love, not courage—his wife, his dignity, his throne, the honour of his father, he forgets them all!'

'Yes,' pursued the Baron, 'the word Abdication. I perceive a glimmering there.'

'I read your fancy,' she returned. 'It is mere madness, midsummer madness. Baron, I am more unpopular than he. You know it. They can excuse, they can love, his weakness; but me, they hate.'

'Such is the gratitude of peoples,' said the Baron. 'But we trifle. Here, madam, are my plain thoughts. The man who in the hour of danger speaks of abdication is, for me, a venomous animal. I speak with the bluntness of gravity, madam; this is no hour for mincing. The coward, in a station of authority, is more dangerous than fire. We dwell on a volcano; if this man can have his way, Grünewald before a week will have been deluged with innocent blood. You know the truth of what I say; we have looked unblenching into this ever-possible catastrophe. To him it is nothing: he will abdicate! Abdicate, just God! and this unhappy country committed to his charge, and the lives of men and the honour of women . . .' His voice appeared to fail him; in an instant he had conquered his emotion and resumed: 'But you, madam, conceive more worthily of your responsibilities. I am with you in the thought; and in the face of the horrors that I see impending, I say, and your heart repeats it—we have gone too far to pause. Honour, duty, ay, and the care of our own lives, demand we should proceed.'

She was looking at him, her brow thoughtfully knitted. 'I feel it,' she said. 'But how? He has the power.'

'The power, madam? The power is in the army,' he replied; and then hastily, ere she could intervene, 'we have to save ourselves,' he went on; 'I have to save my Princess, she has to save her minister; we have both of us to save this infatuated youth from his own madness. He in the outbreak would be the earliest victim; I see him,' he cried, 'torn in pieces; and Grünewald, unhappy Grünewald! Nay, madam, you who have the power must use it; it lies hard upon your conscience.'

'Show me how!' she cried. 'Suppose I were to place him under some constraint, the revolution would break upon us instantly.'

The Baron feigned defeat. 'It is true,' he said. 'You see more clearly than I do. Yet there should, there must be, some way.' And he waited for his chance.

'No,' she said; 'I told you from the first there is no remedy. Our hopes are lost: lost by one miserable trifler, ignorant, fretful, fitful—who will have disappeared to-morrow, who knows? to his boorish pleasures!'

Any peg would do for Gondremark. 'The thing!' he cried, striking his brow. 'Fool, not to have thought of it! Madam, without perhaps knowing it, you have solved our problem.'

'What do you mean? Speak!' she said.

He appeared to collect himself; and then, with a smile, 'The Prince,' he said, 'must go once more a-hunting.'

'Ay, if he would!' cried she, 'and stay there!'

'And stay there,' echoed the Baron. It was so significantly said, that her face changed; and the schemer, fearful of the sinister ambiguity of his expressions, hastened to explain. 'This time he shall go hunting in a carriage, with a good escort of our foreign lancers. His destination shall be the Felsenburg; it is healthy, the rock is high, the windows are small and barred; it might have been built on purpose. We shall intrust the captaincy to the Scotsman Gordon; he at least will have no scruple. Who will miss the sovereign? He is gone hunting; he came home on Tuesday, on Thursday he returned; all is usual in that. Meanwhile the war proceeds; our Prince will soon weary of his solitude; and about the time of our triumph, or, if he prove very obstinate, a little later, he shall be released upon a proper understanding, and I see him once more directing his theatricals.'

Seraphina sat gloomy, plunged in thought. 'Yes,' she said suddenly, 'and the despatch? He is now writing it.'

'It cannot pass the council before Friday,' replied Gondremark; 'and as for any private note, the messengers are all at my disposal. They are picked men, madam. I am a person of precaution.'

'It would appear so,' she said, with a flash of her occasional repugnance to the man; and then after a pause, 'Herr von Gondremark,' she added, 'I recoil from this extremity.'

'I share your Highness's repugnance,' answered he. 'But what would you have? We are defenceless, else.'

'I see it, but this is sudden. It is a public crime,' she said, nodding at him with a sort of horror.

'Look but a little deeper,' he returned, 'and whose is the crime?'

'His!' she cried. 'His, before God! And I hold him liable. But still—'

'It is not as if he would be harmed,' submitted Gondremark.

'I know it,' she replied, but it was still unheartily.

And then, as brave men are entitled, by prescriptive right as old as the world's history, to the alliance and the active help of Fortune, the punctual goddess stepped down from the machine. One of the Princess's ladies begged to enter; a man, it appeared, had brought a line for the Freiherr von Gondremark. It proved to be a pencil billet, which the crafty Greisengesang had found the means to scribble and despatch under the very guns of Otto; and the daring of the act bore testimony to the terror of the actor. For Greisengesang had but one influential motive: fear. The note ran thus: 'At the first council, procuration to be withdrawn.—CORN. GREIS.'

So, after three years of exercise, the right of signature was to be stript from Seraphina. It was more than an insult; it was a public disgrace; and she did not pause to consider how she had earned it, but morally bounded under the attack as bounds the wounded tiger.

'Enough,' she said; 'I will sign the order. When shall he leave?'

'It will take me twelve hours to collect my men, and it had best be done at night. To-morrow midnight, if you please?' answered the Baron.

'Excellent,' she said. 'My door is always open to you, Baron. As soon as the order is prepared, bring it me to sign.'

'Madam,' he said, 'alone of all of us you do not risk your head in this adventure. For that reason, and to prevent all hesitation, I venture to propose the order should be in your hand throughout.'

'You are right,' she replied.

He laid a form before her, and she wrote the order in a clear hand, and re-read it. Suddenly a cruel smile came on her face. 'I had forgotten his puppet,' said she. 'They will keep each other company.' And she interlined and initiated the condemnation of Doctor Gotthold.

'Your Highness has more memory than your servant,' said the Baron; and then he, in his turn, carefully perused the fateful paper. 'Good!' said he.

'You will appear in the drawing-room, Baron?' she asked.

'I thought it better,' said he, 'to avoid the possibility of a public affront. Anything that shook my credit might hamper us in the immediate future.'

'You are right,' she said; and she held out her hand as to an old friend and equal.

CHAPTER IX
THE PRICE OF THE RIVER FARM; IN WHICH VAINGLORY GOES BEFORE A FALL

The pistol had been practically fired. Under ordinary circumstances the scene at the council table would have entirely exhausted Otto's store both of energy and anger; he would have begun to examine and condemn his conduct, have remembered all that was true, forgotten all that was unjust in Seraphina's onslaught; and by half an hour after would have fallen into that state of mind in which a Catholic flees to the confessional and a sot takes refuge with the bottle. Two matters of detail preserved his spirits. For, first, he had still an infinity of business to transact; and to transact business, for a man of Otto's neglectful and procrastinating habits, is the best anodyne for conscience. All afternoon he was hard at it with the Chancellor, reading, dictating, signing, and despatching papers; and this kept him in a glow of self-approval. But, secondly, his vanity was still alarmed; he had failed to get the money; to-morrow before noon he would have to disappoint old Killian; and in the eyes of that family which counted him so little, and to which he had sought to play the part of the heroic comforter, he must sink lower than at first. To a man of Otto's temper, this was death. He could not accept the situation. And even as he worked, and worked wisely and well, over the hated details of his principality, he was secretly maturing a plan by which to turn the situation. It was a scheme as pleasing to the man as it was dishonourable in the prince; in which his frivolous nature found and took vengeance for the gravity and burthen of the afternoon. He chuckled as he thought of it: and Greisengesang heard him with wonder, and attributed his lively spirits to the skirmish of the morning.

Led by this idea, the antique courtier ventured to compliment his sovereign on his bearing. It reminded him, he said, of Otto's father.

'What?' asked the Prince, whose thoughts were miles away.

'Your Highness's authority at the board,' explained the flatterer.

'O, that! O yes,' returned Otto; but for all his carelessness, his vanity was delicately tickled, and his mind returned and dwelt approvingly over the details of his victory. 'I quelled them all,' he thought.

When the more pressing matters had been dismissed, it was already late, and Otto kept the Chancellor to dinner, and was entertained with a leash of ancient histories and modern compliments. The Chancellor's career had been based, from the first off-put, on entire subserviency; he had crawled into honours and employments; and his mind was prostitute. The instinct of the creature served him well with Otto. First, he let fall a sneering word or two upon the female intellect; thence he proceeded to a closer engagement; and before the third course he was artfully dissecting Seraphina's character to her approving husband. Of course no names were used; and of course the identity of that abstract or ideal man, with whom she was currently contrasted, remained an open secret. But this stiff old gentleman had a wonderful instinct for evil, thus to wind his way into man's citadel; thus to harp by the hour on the virtues of his hearer and not once alarm his self-respect. Otto was all roseate, in and out, with flattery and Tokay and an approving conscience. He saw himself in the most attractive colours. If even Greisengesang, he thought, could thus espy the loose stitches in Seraphina's character, and thus disloyally impart them to the opposite camp, he, the discarded husband—the dispossessed Prince—could scarce have erred on the side of severity.

In this excellent frame he bade adieu to the old gentleman, whose voice had proved so musical, and set forth for the drawing-room. Already on the stair, he was seized with some compunction; but when he entered the great gallery and beheld his wife, the Chancellor's abstract flatteries fell from him like rain, and he re-awoke to the poetic facts of life. She stood a good way off below a shining lustre, her back turned. The bend of her waist overcame him with physical weakness. This was the girl-wife who had lain in his arms and whom he had sworn to cherish; there was she, who was better than success.

It was Seraphina who restored him from the blow. She swam forward and smiled upon her husband with a sweetness that was insultingly artificial. 'Frédéric,' she lisped, 'you are late.' It was a scene of high comedy, such as is proper to unhappy marriages; and her *aplomb* disgusted him.

There was no etiquette at these small drawing-rooms. People came and went at pleasure. The window embrasures became the roost of happy couples; at the great chimney the talkers mostly congregated, each full-charged with scandal; and down at the farther end the gamblers gambled. It was towards this point that Otto moved, not ostentatiously, but with a gentle insistence, and scattering attentions as he went. Once abreast of the card-table, he placed himself opposite to Madame von Rosen, and, as soon as he had caught her eye, withdrew to the embrasure of a window. There she had speedily joined him.

'You did well to call me,' she said, a little wildly. 'These cards will be my ruin.'

'Leave them,' said Otto.

'I!' she cried, and laughed; 'they are my destiny. My only chance was to die of a consumption; now I must die in a garret.'

'You are bitter to-night,' said Otto.

'I have been losing,' she replied. 'You do not know what greed is.'

'I have come, then, in an evil hour,' said he.

'Ah, you wish a favour!' she cried, brightening beautifully.

'Madam,' said he, 'I am about to found my party, and I come to you for a recruit.'

'Done,' said the Countess. 'I am a man again.'

'I may be wrong,' continued Otto, 'but I believe upon my heart you wish me no ill.'

'I wish you so well,' she said, 'that I dare not tell it you.'

'Then if I ask my favour?' quoth the Prince.

'Ask it, *mon Prince*,' she answered. 'Whatever it is, it is granted.'

'I wish you,' he returned, 'this very night to make the farmer of our talk.'

'Heaven knows your meaning!' she exclaimed. 'I know not, neither care; there are no bounds to my desire to please you. Call him made.'

'I will put it in another way,' returned Otto. 'Did you ever steal?'

'Often!' cried the Countess. 'I have broken all the ten commandments; and if there were more to-morrow, I should not sleep till I had broken these.'

'This is a case of burglary: to say the truth, I thought it would amuse you,' said the Prince.

'I have no practical experience,' she replied, 'but O! the good-will! I have broken a work-box in my time, and several hearts, my own included. Never a house! But it cannot be difficult; sins are so unromantically easy! What are we to break?'

'Madam, we are to break the treasury,' said Otto and he sketched to her briefly, wittily, with here and there a touch of pathos, the story of his visit to the farm, of his promise to buy it, and of the refusal with which his demand for money had been met that morning at the council; concluding with a few practical words as to the treasury windows, and the helps and hindrances of the proposed exploit.

'They refused you the money,' she said when he had done. 'And you accepted the refusal? Well!'

'They gave their reasons,' replied Otto, colouring. 'They were not such as I could combat; and I am driven to dilapidate the funds of my own country by a theft. It is not dignified; but it is fun.'

'Fun,' she said; 'yes.' And then she remained silently plunged in thought for an appreciable time. 'How much do you require?' she asked at length.

'Three thousand crowns will do,' he answered, 'for I have still some money of my own.'

'Excellent,' she said, regaining her levity. 'I am your true accomplice. And where are we to meet?'

'You know the Flying Mercury,' he answered, 'in the Park? Three pathways intersect; there they have made a seat and raised the statue. The spot is handy and the deity congenial.'

'Child,' she said, and tapped him with her fan. 'But do you know, my Prince, you are an egoist—your handy trysting-place is miles from me. You must give me ample time; I cannot, I think, possibly be there before two. But as the bell beats two, your helper shall arrive: welcome, I trust. Stay—do you bring any one?' she added. 'O, it is not for a chaperon—I am not a prude!'

'I shall bring a groom of mine,' said Otto. 'I caught him stealing corn.'

'His name?' she asked.

'I profess I know not. I am not yet intimate with my corn-stealer,' returned the Prince. 'It was in a professional capacity—'

'Like me! Flatterer!' she cried. 'But oblige me in one thing. Let me find you waiting at the seat—yes, you shall await me; for on this expedition it shall be no longer Prince and Countess, it shall be the lady and the squire—and your friend the thief shall be no nearer than the fountain. Do you promise?'

'Madam, in everything you are to command; you shall be captain, I am but supercargo,' answered Otto.

'Well, Heaven bring all safe to port!' she said. 'It is not Friday!'

Something in her manner had puzzled Otto, had possibly touched him with suspicion.

'Is it not strange,' he remarked, 'that I should choose my accomplice from the other camp?'

'Fool!' she said. 'But it is your only wisdom that you know your friends.' And suddenly, in the vantage of the deep window, she caught up his hand and kissed it with a sort of passion. 'Now go,' she added, 'go at once.'

He went, somewhat staggered, doubting in his heart that he was over-bold. For in that moment she had flashed upon him like a jewel; and even through the strong panoply of a previous love he had been conscious of a shock. Next moment he had dismissed the fear.

Both Otto and the Countess retired early from the drawing-room; and the Prince, after an elaborate feint, dismissed his valet, and went forth by the private passage and the back postern in quest of the groom.

Once more the stable was in darkness, once more Otto employed the talismanic knock, and once more the groom appeared and sickened with terror.

'Good-evening, friend,' said Otto pleasantly. 'I want you to bring a corn sack—empty this time—and to accompany me. We shall be gone all night.'

'Your Highness,' groaned the man, 'I have the charge of the small stables. I am here alone.'

'Come,' said the Prince, 'you are no such martinet in duty.' And then seeing that the man was shaking from head to foot, Otto laid a hand upon his shoulder. 'If I meant you harm,' he said, 'should I be here?'

The fellow became instantly reassured. He got the sack; and Otto led him round by several paths and avenues, conversing pleasantly by the way, and left him at last planted by a certain fountain where a goggle-eyed Triton spouted intermittently into a rippling laver. Thence he proceeded alone to where, in a round clearing, a copy of Gian Bologna's Mercury stood tiptoe in the twilight of the stars. The night was warm and windless. A shaving of new moon had lately arisen; but it was still too small and too low down in heaven to contend with the immense host of lesser luminaries; and the rough face of the earth was drenched with starlight. Down one of the alleys, which widened as it receded, he could see a part of the lamplit terrace where a sentry silently paced, and beyond that a corner of the town with interlacing street-lights. But all around him the young trees stood mystically blurred in the dim shine; and in the stock-still quietness the upleaping god appeared alive.

In this dimness and silence of the night, Otto's conscience became suddenly and staringly luminous, like the dial of a city clock. He averted the eyes of his mind, but the finger rapidly travelling, pointed to a series of misdeeds that took his breath away. What was he doing in that place? The money had been wrongly squandered, but that was largely by his own neglect. And he now proposed to embarrass the finances of this country which he had been too idle to govern. And he now proposed to squander the money once again, and this time for a private, if a generous end. And the man whom he had reproved for stealing corn he was now to set stealing treasure. And then there was Madame von Rosen, upon whom he looked down with some of that ill-favoured contempt of the chaste male for the imperfect woman. Because he thought of her as one degraded below scruples, he had picked her out to be still more degraded, and to risk her whole irregular establishment in life by complicity in this dishonourable act. It was uglier than a seduction.

Otto had to walk very briskly and whistle very busily; and when at last he heard steps in the narrowest and darkest of the alleys, it was with a gush of relief that he sprang to meet the Countess. To wrestle alone with one's good angel is so hard! and so precious, at the proper time, is a companion certain to be less virtuous than oneself!

It was a young man who came towards him—a young man of small stature and a peculiar gait, wearing a wide flapping hat, and carrying, with great weariness, a heavy bag. Otto recoiled; but the young man held up his hand by way of signal, and coming up with a panting run, as if with the last of his endurance, laid the bag upon the ground, threw himself upon the bench, and disclosed the features of Madame von Rosen.

'You, Countess!' cried the Prince.

'No, no,' she panted, 'the Count von Rosen—my young brother. A capital fellow. Let him get his breath.'

'Ah, madam . . . ' said he.

'Call me Count,' she returned, 'respect my incognito.'

'Count be it, then,' he replied. 'And let me implore that gallant gentleman to set forth at once on our enterprise.'

'Sit down beside me here,' she returned, patting the further corner of the bench. 'I will follow you in a moment. O, I am so tired—feel how my heart leaps! Where is your thief?'

'At his post,' replied Otto. 'Shall I introduce him? He seems an excellent companion.'

'No,' she said, 'do not hurry me yet. I must speak to you. Not but I adore your thief; I adore any one who has the spirit to do wrong. I never cared for virtue till I fell in love with my Prince.' She laughed musically. 'And even so, it is not for your virtues,' she added.

Otto was embarrassed. 'And now,' he asked, 'if you are anyway rested?'

'Presently, presently. Let me breathe,' she said, panting a little harder than before.

'And what has so wearied you?' he asked. 'This bag? And why, in the name of eccentricity, a bag? For an empty one, you might have relied on my own foresight; and this one is very far from being empty. My dear Count, with what trash have you come laden? But the shortest method is to see for myself.' And he put down his hand.

She stopped him at once. 'Otto,' she said, 'no—not that way. I will tell, I will make a clean breast. It is done already. I have robbed the treasury single-handed. There are three thousand two hundred crowns. O, I trust it is enough!'

Her embarrassment was so obvious that the Prince was struck into a muse, gazing in her face, with his hand still outstretched, and she still holding him by the wrist. 'You!' he said at last. 'How?' And then drawing himself up, 'O madam,' he cried, 'I understand. You must indeed think meanly of the Prince.'

'Well, then, it was a lie!' she cried. 'The money is mine, honestly my own— now yours. This was an unworthy act that you proposed. But I love your honour, and I swore to myself that I should save it in your teeth. I beg of you to let me save it'—with a sudden lovely change of tone. 'Otto, I beseech you let me save it. Take this dross from your poor friend who loves you!'

'Madam, madam,' babbled Otto, in the extreme of misery, 'I cannot—I must go.'

And he half rose; but she was on the ground before him in an instant, clasping his knees. 'No,' she gasped, 'you shall not go. Do you despise me so entirely? It is dross; I hate it; I should squander it at play and be no richer; it is an investment, it is to save me from ruin. Otto,' she cried, as he again feebly tried to put her from him, 'if you leave me alone in this disgrace, I will die here!' He groaned aloud. 'O,' she said, 'think what I suffer! If you suffer from a piece of delicacy, think what I suffer in my shame! To have my trash refused! You would rather steal, you think of me so basely! You would rather tread my heart in pieces! O, unkind! O my Prince! O Otto! O pity me!' She was still clasping him; then she found his hand and covered it with kisses, and at this his head began to turn. 'O,' she cried again, 'I see it! O what a horror! It is because I am old, because I am no longer beautiful.' And she burst into a storm of sobs.

This was the *coup de grâce*. Otto had now to comfort and compose her as he could, and before many words, the money was accepted. Between the woman and the weak man such was the inevitable end. Madame von

Rosen instantly composed her sobs. She thanked him with a fluttering voice, and resumed her place upon the bench, at the far end from Otto. 'Now you see,' she said, 'why I bade you keep the thief at distance, and why I came alone. How I trembled for my treasure!'

'Madam,' said Otto, with a tearful whimper in his voice, 'spare me! You are too good, too noble!'

'I wonder to hear you,' she returned. 'You have avoided a great folly. You will be able to meet your good old peasant. You have found an excellent investment for a friend's money. You have preferred essential kindness to an empty scruple; and now you are ashamed of it! You have made your friend happy; and now you mourn as the dove! Come, cheer up. I know it is depressing to have done exactly right; but you need not make a practice of it. Forgive yourself this virtue; come now, look me in the face and smile!'

He did look at her. When a man has been embraced by a woman, he sees her in a glamour; and at such a time, in the baffling glimmer of the stars, she will look wildly well. The hair is touched with light; the eyes are constellations; the face sketched in shadows—a sketch, you might say, by passion. Otto became consoled for his defeat; he began to take an interest. 'No,' he said, 'I am no ingrate.'

'You promised me fun,' she returned, with a laugh. 'I have given you as good. We have had a stormy *scena*.'

He laughed in his turn, and the sound of the laughter, in either case, was hardly reassuring.

'Come, what are you going to give me in exchange,' she continued, 'for my excellent declamation?'

'What you will,' he said.

'Whatever I will? Upon your honour? Suppose I asked the crown?' She was flashing upon him, beautiful in triumph.

'Upon my honour,' he replied.

'Shall I ask the crown?' she continued. 'Nay; what should I do with it? Grünewald is but a petty state; my ambition swells above it. I shall ask—I find I want nothing,' she concluded. 'I will give you something instead. I will give you leave to kiss me—once.'

Otto drew near, and she put up her face; they were both smiling, both on the brink of laughter, all was so innocent and playful; and the Prince, when their lips encountered, was dumbfounded by the sudden convulsion of his being. Both drew instantly apart, and for an appreciable time sat tongue-tied. Otto was indistinctly conscious of a peril in the silence, but could find no words to utter. Suddenly the Countess seemed to awake. 'As for your wife—' she began in a clear and steady voice.

The word recalled Otto, with a shudder, from his trance. 'I will hear nothing against my wife,' he cried wildly; and then, recovering himself and in a kindlier tone, 'I will tell you my one secret,' he added. 'I love my wife.'

'You should have let me finish,' she returned, smiling. 'Do you suppose I did not mention her on purpose? You know you had lost your head. Well, so had I. Come now, do not be abashed by words,' she added somewhat sharply. 'It is the one thing I despise. If you are not a fool, you will see that I am building fortresses about your virtue. And at any rate, I choose that you shall understand that I am not dying of love for you. It is a very smiling business; no tragedy for me! And now here is what I have to say about your wife; she is not and she never has been Gondremark's mistress. Be sure he would have boasted if she had. Good-night!'

And in a moment she was gone down the alley, and Otto was alone with the bag of money and the flying god.

CHAPTER X
GOTTHOLD'S REVISED OPINION; AND THE FALL COMPLETED

The Countess left poor Otto with a caress and buffet simultaneously administered. The welcome word about his wife and the virtuous ending of his interview should doubtless have delighted him. But for all that, as he shouldered the bag of money and set forward to rejoin his groom, he was conscious of many aching sensibilities. To have gone wrong and to have been set right makes but a double trial for man's vanity. The discovery of his own weakness and possible unfaith had staggered him to the heart; and to hear, in the same hour, of his wife's fidelity from one who loved her not, increased the bitterness of the surprise.

He was about half-way between the fountain and the Flying Mercury before his thoughts began to be clear; and he was surprised to find them resentful. He paused in a kind of temper, and struck with his hand a little shrub. Thence there arose instantly a cloud of awakened sparrows, which as instantly dispersed and disappeared into the thicket. He looked at them stupidly, and when they were gone continued staring at the stars. 'I am angry. By what right? By none!' he thought; but he was still angry. He cursed Madame von Rosen and instantly repented. Heavy was the money on his shoulders.

When he reached the fountain, he did, out of ill-humour and parade, an unpardonable act. He gave the money bodily to the dishonest groom. 'Keep this for me,' he said, 'until I call for it to-morrow. It is a great sum, and by that you will judge that I have not condemned you.' And he strode away ruffling, as if he had done something generous. It was a desperate stroke to re-enter at the point of the bayonet into his self-esteem; and, like all such, it was fruitless in the end. He got to bed with the devil, it appeared: kicked and tumbled till the grey of the morning; and then fell inopportunely into a leaden slumber, and awoke to find it ten. To miss the appointment with old Killian after all, had been too tragic a miscarriage: and he hurried with all his might, found the groom (for a wonder) faithful to his trust, and arrived only a few minutes before noon in the guest-chamber of the Morning Star. Killian was there in his Sunday's best and looking very gaunt and rigid; a lawyer from Brandenau stood sentinel over his outspread papers; and the groom and the landlord of the inn were called to serve as witnesses. The obvious deference of that great man, the innkeeper, plainly affected the old farmer with surprise; but it was not until

Otto had taken the pen and signed that the truth flashed upon him fully. Then, indeed, he was beside himself.

'His Highness!' he cried, 'His Highness!' and repeated the exclamation till his mind had grappled fairly with the facts. Then he turned to the witnesses. 'Gentlemen,' he said, 'you dwell in a country highly favoured by God; for of all generous gentlemen, I will say it on my conscience, this one is the king. I am an old man, and I have seen good and bad, and the year of the great famine; but a more excellent gentleman, no, never.'

'We know that,' cried the landlord, 'we know that well in Grünewald. If we saw more of his Highness we should be the better pleased.'

'It is the kindest Prince,' began the groom, and suddenly closed his mouth upon a sob, so that every one turned to gaze upon his emotion—Otto not last; Otto struck with remorse, to see the man so grateful.

Then it was the lawyer's turn to pay a compliment. 'I do not know what Providence may hold in store,' he said, 'but this day should be a bright one in the annals of your reign. The shouts of armies could not be more eloquent than the emotion on these honest faces.' And the Brandenau lawyer bowed, skipped, stepped back, and took snuff, with the air of a man who has found and seized an opportunity.

'Well, young gentleman,' said Killian, 'if you will pardon me the plainness of calling you a gentleman, many a good day's work you have done, I doubt not, but never a better, or one that will be better blessed; and whatever, sir, may be your happiness and triumph in that high sphere to which you have been called, it will be none the worse, sir, for an old man's blessing!'

The scene had almost assumed the proportions of an ovation; and when the Prince escaped he had but one thought: to go wherever he was most sure of praise. His conduct at the board of council occurred to him as a fair chapter; and this evoked the memory of Gotthold. To Gotthold he would go.

Gotthold was in the library as usual, and laid down his pen, a little angrily, on Otto's entrance. 'Well,' he said, 'here you are.'

'Well,' returned Otto, 'we made a revolution, I believe.'

'It is what I fear,' returned the Doctor.

'How?' said Otto. 'Fear? Fear is the burnt child. I have learned my strength and the weakness of the others; and I now mean to govern.'

Gotthold said nothing, but he looked down and smoothed his chin.

'You disapprove?' cried Otto. 'You are a weather-cock.'

'On the contrary,' replied the Doctor. 'My observation has confirmed my fears. It will not do, Otto, not do.'

'What will not do?' demanded the Prince, with a sickening stab of pain.

'None of it,' answered Gotthold. 'You are unfitted for a life of action; you lack the stamina, the habit, the restraint, the patience. Your wife is greatly better, vastly better; and though she is in bad hands, displays a very different aptitude. She is a woman of affairs; you are—dear boy, you are yourself. I bid you back to your amusements; like a smiling dominie, I give you holidays for life. Yes,' he continued, 'there is a day appointed for all when they shall turn again upon their own philosophy. I had grown to disbelieve impartially in all; and if in the atlas of the sciences there were two charts I disbelieved in more than all the rest, they were politics and morals. I had a sneaking kindness for your vices; as they were negative, they flattered my philosophy; and I called them almost virtues. Well, Otto, I was wrong; I have forsworn my sceptical philosophy; and I perceive your faults to be unpardonable. You are unfit to be a Prince, unfit to be a husband. And I give you my word, I would rather see a man capably doing evil than blundering about good.'

Otto was still silent, in extreme dudgeon.

Presently the Doctor resumed: 'I will take the smaller matter first: your conduct to your wife. You went, I hear, and had an explanation. That may have been right or wrong; I know not; at least, you had stirred her temper. At the council she insults you; well, you insult her back—a man to a woman, a husband to his wife, in public! Next upon the back of this, you propose—the story runs like wildfire—to recall the power of signature. Can she ever forgive that? a woman—a young woman—ambitious, conscious of talents beyond yours? Never, Otto. And to sum all, at such a crisis in your married life, you get into a window corner with that ogling dame von Rosen. I do not dream that there was any harm; but I do say it was an idle disrespect to your wife. Why, man, the woman is not decent.'

'Gotthold,' said Otto, 'I will hear no evil of the Countess.'

'You will certainly hear no good of her,' returned Gotthold; 'and if you wish your wife to be the pink of nicety, you should clear your court of demi-reputations.'

'The commonplace injustice of a by-word,' Otto cried. 'The partiality of sex. She is a demirep; what then is Gondremark? Were she a man—'

'It would be all one,' retorted Gotthold roughly. 'When I see a man, come to years of wisdom, who speaks in double-meanings and is the braggart of his vices, I spit on the other side. "You, my friend," say I, "are not even a gentleman." Well, she's not even a lady.'

'She is the best friend I have, and I choose that she shall be respected,' Otto said.

'If she is your friend, so much the worse,' replied the Doctor. 'It will not stop there.'

'Ah!' cried Otto, 'there is the charity of virtue! All evil in the spotted fruit. But I can tell you, sir, that you do Madame von Rosen prodigal injustice.'

'You can tell me!' said the Doctor shrewdly. 'Have you, tried? have you been riding the marches?'

The blood came into Otto's face.

'Ah!' cried Gotthold, 'look at your wife and blush! There's a wife for a man to marry and then lose! She's a carnation, Otto. The soul is in her eyes.'

'You have changed your note for Seraphina, I perceive,' said Otto.

'Changed it!' cried the Doctor, with a flush. 'Why, when was it different? But I own I admired her at the council. When she sat there silent, tapping with her foot, I admired her as I might a hurricane. Were I one of those who venture upon matrimony, there had been the prize to tempt me! She invites, as Mexico invited Cortez; the enterprise is hard, the natives are unfriendly—I believe them cruel too—but the metropolis is paved with gold and the breeze blows out of paradise. Yes, I could desire to be that conqueror. But to philander with von Rosen! never! Senses? I discard them; what are they?—pruritus! Curiosity? Reach me my Anatomy!'

'To whom do you address yourself?' cried Otto. 'Surely you, of all men, know that I love my wife!'

'O, love!' cried Gotthold; 'love is a great word; it is in all the dictionaries. If you had loved, she would have paid you back. What does she ask? A little ardour!'

'It is hard to love for two,' replied the Prince.

'Hard? Why, there's the touchstone! O, I know my poets!' cried the Doctor. 'We are but dust and fire, too and to endure life's scorching; and love, like the shadow of a great rock, should lend shelter and refreshment, not to the lover only, but to his mistress and to the children that reward them; and their very friends should seek repose in the fringes of that peace. Love is not love that cannot build a home. And you call it love to grudge and quarrel and pick faults? You call it love to thwart her to her face, and bandy insults? Love!'

'Gotthold, you are unjust. I was then fighting for my country,' said the Prince.

'Ay, and there's the worst of all,' returned the Doctor. 'You could not even see that you were wrong; that being where they were, retreat was ruin.'

Why, you supported me!' cried Otto.

'I did. I was a fool like you,' replied Gotthold. 'But now my eyes are open. If you go on as you have started, disgrace this fellow Gondremark, and publish the scandal of your divided house, there will befall a most abominable thing in Grünewald. A revolution, friend—a revolution.'

'You speak strangely for a red,' said Otto.

'A red republican, but not a revolutionary,' returned the Doctor. 'An ugly thing is a Grünewalder drunk! One man alone can save the country from this pass, and that is the double-dealer Gondremark, with whom I conjure you to make peace. It will not be you; it never can be you:—you, who can do nothing, as your wife said, but trade upon your station—you, who spent the hours in begging money! And in God's name, what for? Why money? What mystery of idiocy was this?'

'It was to no ill end. It was to buy a farm,' quoth Otto sulkily.

'To buy a farm!' cried Gotthold. 'Buy a farm!'

'Well, what then?' returned Otto. 'I have bought it, if you come to that.'

Gotthold fairly bounded on his seat. 'And how that?' he cried.

'How?' repeated Otto, startled.

'Ay, verily, how!' returned the Doctor. 'How came you by the money?'

The Prince's countenance darkened. 'That is my affair,' said he.

'You see you are ashamed,' retorted Gotthold. 'And so you bought a farm in the hour of our country's need—doubtless to be ready for the abdication; and I put it that you stole the funds. There are not three ways of getting money: there are but two: to earn and steal. And now, when you have combined Charles the Fifth and Long-fingered Tom, you come to me to fortify your vanity! But I will clear my mind upon this matter: until I know the right and wrong of the transaction, I put my hand behind my back. A man may be the pitifullest prince; he must be a spotless gentleman.'

The Prince had gotten to his feet, as pale as paper. Gotthold,' he said, 'you drive me beyond bounds. Beware, sir, beware!'

'Do you threaten me, friend Otto?' asked the Doctor grimly. 'That would be a strange conclusion.'

'When have you ever known me use my power in any private animosity?' cried Otto. 'To any private man your words were an unpardonable insult, but at me you shoot in full security, and I must turn aside to compliment you on your plainness. I must do more than pardon, I must admire, because you have faced this—this formidable monarch, like a Nathan before David. You have uprooted an old kindness, sir, with an unsparing hand. You leave me very bare. My last bond is broken; and though I take Heaven to witness that I sought to do the right, I have this reward: to find myself alone. You say I am no gentleman; yet the sneers have been upon your side; and though I can very well perceive where you have lodged your sympathies, I will forbear the taunt.'

'Otto, are you insane?' cried Gotthold, leaping up. 'Because I ask you how you came by certain moneys, and because you refuse—'

'Herr von Hohenstockwitz, I have ceased to invite your aid in my affairs,' said Otto. 'I have heard all that I desire, and you have sufficiently trampled on my vanity. It may be that I cannot govern, it may be that I cannot love—you tell me so with every mark of honesty; but God has granted me one virtue, and I can still forgive. I forgive you; even in this hour of passion, I can perceive my faults and your excuses; and if I desire that in future I may be spared your conversation, it is not, sir, from resentment— not resentment—but, by Heaven, because no man on earth could endure to be so rated. You have the satisfaction to see your sovereign weep; and that person whom you have so often taunted with his happiness reduced to the last pitch of solitude and misery. No,—I will hear nothing; I claim the last word, sir, as your Prince; and that last word shall be—forgiveness.'

And with that Otto was gone from the apartment, and Doctor Gotthold was left alone with the most conflicting sentiments of sorrow, remorse, and merriment; walking to and fro before his table, and asking himself, with hands uplifted, which of the pair of them was most to blame for this unhappy rupture. Presently, he took from a cupboard a bottle of Rhine wine and a goblet of the deep Bohemian ruby. The first glass a little warmed and comforted his bosom; with the second he began to look down upon these troubles from a sunny mountain; yet a while, and filled with this false comfort and contemplating life throughout a golden medium, he owned to himself, with a flush, a smile, and a half-pleasurable sigh, that he had been somewhat over plain in dealing with his cousin. 'He said the truth, too,' added the penitent librarian, 'for in my monkish fashion I adore the Princess.' And then, with a still deepening flush and a certain stealth, although he sat all alone in that great gallery, he toasted Seraphina to the dregs.

CHAPTER XI
PROVIDENCE VON ROSEN: ACT THE FIRST
SHE BEGUILES THE BARON

At a sufficiently late hour, or to be more exact, at three in the afternoon, Madame von Rosen issued on the world. She swept downstairs and out across the garden, a black mantilla thrown over her head, and the long train of her black velvet dress ruthlessly sweeping in the dirt.

At the other end of that long garden, and back to back with the villa of the Countess, stood the large mansion where the Prime Minister transacted his affairs and pleasures. This distance, which was enough for decency by the easy canons of Mittwalden, the Countess swiftly traversed, opened a little door with a key, mounted a flight of stairs, and entered unceremoniously into Gondremark's study. It was a large and very high apartment; books all about the walls, papers on the table, papers on the floor; here and there a picture, somewhat scant of drapery; a great fire glowing and flaming in the blue tiled hearth; and the daylight streaming through a cupola above. In the midst of this sat the great Baron Gondremark in his shirt-sleeves, his business for that day fairly at an end, and the hour arrived for relaxation. His expression, his very nature, seemed to have undergone a fundamental change. Gondremark at home appeared the very antipode of Gondremark on duty. He had an air of massive jollity that well became him; grossness and geniality sat upon his features; and along with his manners, he had laid aside his sly and sinister expression. He lolled there, sunning his bulk before the fire, a noble animal.

'Hey!' he cried. 'At last!'

The Countess stepped into the room in silence, threw herself on a chair, and crossed her legs. In her lace and velvet, with a good display of smooth black stocking and of snowy petticoat, and with the refined profile of her face and slender plumpness of her body, she showed in singular contrast to the big, black, intellectual satyr by the fire.

'How often do you send for me?' she cried. 'It is compromising.'

Gondremark laughed. 'Speaking of that,' said he, 'what in the devil's name were you about? You were not home till morning.'

'I was giving alms,' she said.

The Baron again laughed loud and long, for in his shirt-sleeves he was a very mirthful creature. 'It is fortunate I am not jealous,' he remarked. 'But you know my way: pleasure and liberty go hand in hand. I believe what I believe; it is not much, but I believe it.—But now to business. Have you not read my letter?'

'No,' she said; 'my head ached.'

'Ah, well! then I have news indeed!' cried Gondremark. 'I was mad to see you all last night and all this morning: for yesterday afternoon I brought my long business to a head; the ship has come home; one more dead lift, and I shall cease to fetch and carry for the Princess Ratafia. Yes, 'tis done. I have the order all in Ratafia's hand; I carry it on my heart. At the hour of twelve to-night, Prince Featherhead is to be taken in his bed and, like the bambino, whipped into a chariot; and by next morning he will command a most romantic prospect from the donjon of the Felsenburg. Farewell, Featherhead! The war goes on, the girl is in my hand; I have long been indispensable, but now I shall be sole. I have long,' he added exultingly, 'long carried this intrigue upon my shoulders, like Samson with the gates of Gaza; now I discharge that burthen.'

She had sprung to her feet a little paler. 'Is this true?' she cried.

'I tell you a fact,' he asseverated. 'The trick is played.'

'I will never believe it,' she said. 'An order in her own hand? I will never believe it, Heinrich.'

'I swear to you,' said he.

'O, what do you care for oaths—or I either? What would you swear by? Wine, women, and song? It is not binding,' she said. She had come quite close up to him and laid her hand upon his arm. 'As for the order—no, Heinrich, never! I will never believe it. I will die ere I believe it. You have some secret purpose—what, I cannot guess—but not one word of it is true.'

'Shall I show it you?' he asked.

'You cannot,' she answered. 'There is no such thing.'

'Incorrigible Sadducee!' he cried. 'Well, I will convert you; you shall see the order.' He moved to a chair where he had thrown his coat, and then drawing forth and holding out a paper, 'Read,' said he.

She took it greedily, and her eye flashed as she perused it.

'Hey!' cried the Baron, 'there falls a dynasty, and it was I that felled it; and I and you inherit!' He seemed to swell in stature; and next moment, with a laugh, he put his hand forward. Give me the dagger,' said he.

But she whisked the paper suddenly behind her back and faced him, lowering. 'No, no,' she said. 'You and I have first a point to settle. Do you suppose me blind? She could never have given that paper but to one man, and that man her lover. Here you stand—her lover, her accomplice, her master—O, I well believe it, for I know your power. But what am I?' she cried; 'I, whom you deceive!'

'Jealousy!' cried Gondremark. 'Anna, I would never have believed it! But I declare to you by all that's credible that I am not her lover. I might be, I suppose; but I never yet durst risk the declaration. The chit is so unreal; a mincing doll; she will and she will not; there is no counting on her, by God! And hitherto I have had my own way without, and keep the lover in reserve. And I say, Anna,' he added with severity, 'you must break yourself of this new fit, my girl; there must be no combustion. I keep the creature under the belief that I adore her; and if she caught a breath of you and me, she is such a fool, prude, and dog in the manger, that she is capable of spoiling all.'

'All very fine,' returned the lady. 'With whom do you pass your days? and which am I to believe, your words or your actions?'

'Anna, the devil take you, are you blind?' cried Gondremark. 'You know me. Am I likely to care for such a preciosa? 'Tis hard that we should have been together for so long, and you should still take me for a troubadour. But if there is one thing that I despise and deprecate, it is all such figures in Berlin wool. Give me a human woman—like myself. You are my mate; you were made for me; you amuse me like the play. And what have I to gain that I should pretend to you? If I do not love you, what use are you to me? Why, none. It is as clear as noonday.'

'Do you love me, Heinrich?' she asked, languishing. 'Do you truly?'

'I tell you,' he cried, 'I love you next after myself. I should be all abroad if I had lost you.'

'Well, then,' said she, folding up the paper and putting it calmly in her pocket, 'I will believe you, and I join the plot. Count upon me. At midnight, did you say? It is Gordon, I see, that you have charged with it. Excellent; he will stick at nothing—'

Gondremark watched her suspiciously. 'Why do you take the paper?' he demanded. 'Give it here.'

'No,' she returned; 'I mean to keep it. It is I who must prepare the stroke; you cannot manage it without me; and to do my best I must possess the paper. Where shall I find Gordon? In his rooms?' She spoke with a rather feverish self-possession.

'Anna,' he said sternly, the black, bilious countenance of his palace *rôle* taking the place of the more open favour of his hours at home, 'I ask you for that paper. Once, twice, and thrice.'

'Heinrich,' she returned, looking him in the face, 'take care. I will put up with no dictation.'

Both looked dangerous; and the silence lasted for a measurable interval of time. Then she made haste to have the first word; and with a laugh that rang clear and honest, 'Do not be a child,' she said. 'I wonder at you. If your assurances are true, you can have no reason to mistrust me, nor I to play you false. The difficulty is to get the Prince out of the palace without scandal. His valets are devoted; his chamberlain a slave; and yet one cry might ruin all.'

'They must be overpowered,' he said, following her to the new ground, 'and disappear along with him.'

'And your whole scheme along with them!' she cried. 'He does not take his servants when he goes a-hunting: a child could read the truth. No, no; the plan is idiotic; it must be Ratafia's. But hear me. You know the Prince worships me?'

'I know,' he said. 'Poor Featherhead, I cross his destiny!'

'Well now,' she continued, 'what if I bring him alone out of the palace, to some quiet corner of the Park—the Flying Mercury, for instance? Gordon can be posted in the thicket; the carriage wait behind the temple; not a cry, not a scuffle, not a footfall; simply, the Prince vanishes!—What do you say? Am I an able ally? Are my *beaux yuex* of service? Ah, Heinrich, do not lose your Anna!—she has power!'

He struck with his open hand upon the chimney. 'Witch!' he said, 'there is not your match for devilry in Europe. Service! the thing runs on wheels.'

'Kiss me, then, and let me go. I must not miss my Featherhead,' she said.

'Stay, stay,' said the Baron; 'not so fast. I wish, upon my soul, that I could trust you; but you are, out and in, so whimsical a devil that I dare not. Hang it, Anna, no; it's not possible!'

'You doubt me, Heinrich?' she cried.

'Doubt is not the word,' said he. 'I know you. Once you were clear of me with that paper in your pocket, who knows what you would do with it?— not you, at least—nor I. You see,' he added, shaking his head paternally upon the Countess, 'you are as vicious as a monkey.'

'I swear to you,' she cried, 'by my salvation . . . '

'I have no curiosity to hear you swearing,' said the Baron.

'You think that I have no religion? You suppose me destitute of honour. Well,' she said, 'see here: I will not argue, but I tell you once for all: leave me this order, and the Prince shall be arrested—take it from me, and, as certain as I speak, I will upset the coach. Trust me, or fear me: take your choice.' And she offered him the paper.

The Baron, in a great contention of mind, stood irresolute, weighing the two dangers. Once his hand advanced, then dropped. 'Well,' he said, 'since trust is what you call it . . .'

'No more,' she interrupted, 'Do not spoil your attitude. And now since you have behaved like a good sort of fellow in the dark, I will condescend to tell you why. I go to the palace to arrange with Gordon; but how is Gordon to obey me? And how can I foresee the hours? It may be midnight; ay, and it may be nightfall; all's a chance; and to act, I must be free and hold the strings of the adventure. And now,' she cried, 'your Vivien goes. Dub me your knight!' And she held out her arms and smiled upon him radiant.

'Well,' he said, when he had kissed her, 'every man must have his folly; I thank God mine is no worse. Off with you! I have given a child a squib.'

CHAPTER XII
PROVIDENCE VON ROSEN: ACT THE
SECOND SHE INFORMS THE PRINCE

It was the first impulse of Madame von Rosen to return to her own villa and revise her toilette. Whatever else should come of this adventure, it was her firm design to pay a visit to the Princess. And before that woman, so little beloved, the Countess would appear at no disadvantage. It was the work of minutes. Von Rosen had the captain's eye in matters of the toilette; she was none of those who hang in Fabian helplessness among their finery and, after hours, come forth upon the world as dowdies. A glance, a loosened curl, a studied and admired disorder in the hair, a bit of lace, a touch of colour, a yellow rose in the bosom; and the instant picture was complete.

'That will do,' she said. 'Bid my carriage follow me to the palace. In half an hour it should be there in waiting.'

The night was beginning to fall and the shops to shine with lamps along the tree-beshadowed thorough-fares of Otto's capital, when the Countess started on her high emprise. She was jocund at heart; pleasure and interest had winged her beauty, and she knew it. She paused before the glowing jeweller's; she remarked and praised a costume in the milliner's window; and when she reached the lime-tree walk, with its high, umbrageous arches and stir of passers-by in the dim alleys, she took her place upon a bench and began to dally with the pleasures of the hour. It was cold, but she did not feel it, being warm within; her thoughts, in that dark corner, shone like the gold and rubies at the jewellers; her ears, which heard the brushing of so many footfalls, transposed it into music.

What was she to do? She held the paper by which all depended. Otto and Gondremark and Ratafia, and the state itself, hung light in her balances, as light as dust; her little finger laid in either scale would set all flying: and she hugged herself upon her huge preponderance, and then laughed aloud to think how giddily it might be used. The vertigo of omnipotence, the disease of Cæsars, shook her reason. 'O the mad world!' she thought, and laughed aloud in exultation.

A child, finger in mouth, had paused a little way from where she sat, and stared with cloudy interest upon this laughing lady. She called it nearer; but the child hung back. Instantly, with that curious passion which you may see any woman in the world display, on the most odd occasions, for a similar end, the Countess bent herself with singleness of mind to overcome this diffidence; and presently, sure enough, the child was seated on her knee, thumbing and glowering at her watch.

'If you had a clay bear and a china monkey,' asked Von Rosen, 'which would you prefer to break?'

'But I have neither,' said the child.

'Well,' she said, 'here is a bright florin, with which you may purchase both the one and the other; and I shall give it you at once, if you will answer my question. The clay bear or the china monkey—come?'

But the unbreeched soothsayer only stared upon the florin with big eyes; the oracle could not be persuaded to reply; and the Countess kissed him lightly, gave him the florin, set him down upon the path, and resumed her way with swinging and elastic gait.

'Which shall I break?' she wondered; and she passed her hand with delight among the careful disarrangement of her locks. 'Which?' and she consulted heaven with her bright eyes. 'Do I love both or neither? A little—passionately—not at all? Both or neither—both, I believe; but at least I will make hay of Ratafia.'

By the time she had passed the iron gates, mounted the drive, and set her foot upon the broad flagged terrace, the night had come completely; the palace front was thick with lighted windows; and along the balustrade, the lamp on every twentieth baluster shone clear. A few withered tracks of sunset, amber and glow-worm green, still lingered in the western sky; and she paused once again to watch them fading.

'And to think,' she said, 'that here am I—destiny embodied, a norn, a fate, a providence—and have no guess upon which side I shall declare myself! What other woman in my place would not be prejudiced, and think herself committed? But, thank Heaven! I was born just!' Otto's windows were bright among the rest, and she looked on them with rising tenderness. 'How does it feel to be deserted?' she thought. 'Poor dear fool! The girl deserves that he should see this order.'

Without more delay, she passed into the palace and asked for an audience of Prince Otto. The Prince, she was told, was in his own apartment, and desired to be private. She sent her name. A man presently returned with word that the Prince tendered his apologies, but could see no one. 'Then I will write,' she said, and scribbled a few lines alleging urgency of life and death. 'Help me, my Prince,' she added; 'none but you can help me.' This time the messenger returned more speedily, and begged the Countess to follow him: the Prince was graciously pleased to receive the Frau Gräfin von Rosen.

Otto sat by the fire in his large armoury, weapons faintly glittering all about him in the changeful light. His face was disfigured by the marks of weeping; he looked sour and sad; nor did he rise to greet his visitor, but bowed, and bade the man begone. That kind of general tenderness which served the Countess for both heart and conscience, sharply smote her at this spectacle of grief and weakness; she began immediately to enter into the spirit of her part; and as soon as they were alone, taking one step forward and with a magnificent gesture—'Up!' she cried.

'Madame von Rosen,' replied Otto dully, 'you have used strong words. You speak of life and death. Pray, madam, who is threatened? Who is there,' he added bitterly, 'so destitute that even Otto of Grünewald can assist him?'

'First learn,' said she, 'the names of the conspirators; the Princess and the Baron Gondremark. Can you not guess the rest?' And then, as he maintained his silence—'You!' she cried, pointing at him with her finger. ''Tis you they threaten! Your rascal and mine have laid their heads together and condemned you. But they reckoned without you and me. We make a *partie carrée*, Prince, in love and politics. They lead an ace, but we shall trump it. Come, partner, shall I draw my card?'

'Madam,' he said, 'explain yourself. Indeed I fail to comprehend.'

'See, then,' said she; and handed him the order.

He took it, looked upon it with a start; and then, still without speech, he put his hand before his face. She waited for a word in vain.

'What!' she cried, 'do you take the thing down-heartedly? As well seek wine in a milk-pail as love in that girl's heart! Be done with this, and be a man. After the league of the lions, let us have a conspiracy of mice, and pull this piece of machinery to ground. You were brisk enough last night when nothing was at stake and all was frolic. Well, here is better sport; here is life indeed.'

He got to his feet with some alacrity, and his face, which was a little flushed, bore the marks of resolution.

'Madame von Rosen,' said he, 'I am neither unconscious nor ungrateful; this is the true continuation of your friendship; but I see that I must disappoint your expectations. You seem to expect from me some effort of resistance; but why should I resist? I have not much to gain; and now that I have read this paper, and the last of a fool's paradise is shattered, it would be hyperbolical to speak of loss in the same breath with Otto of

Grünewald. I have no party, no policy; no pride, nor anything to be proud of. For what benefit or principle under Heaven do you expect me to contend? Or would you have me bite and scratch like a trapped weasel? No, madam; signify to those who sent you my readiness to go. I would at least avoid a scandal.'

'You go?—of your own will, you go?' she cried.

'I cannot say so much, perhaps,' he answered; 'but I go with good alacrity. I have desired a change some time; behold one offered me! Shall I refuse? Thank God, I am not so destitute of humour as to make a tragedy of such a farce.' He flicked the order on the table. 'You may signify my readiness,' he added grandly.

'Ah,' she said, 'you are more angry than you own.'

'I, madam? angry?' he cried. 'You rave! I have no cause for anger. In every way I have been taught my weakness, my instability, and my unfitness for the world. I am a plexus of weaknesses, an impotent Prince, a doubtful gentleman; and you yourself, indulgent as you are, have twice reproved my levity. And shall I be angry? I may feel the unkindness, but I have sufficient honesty of mind to see the reasons of this *coup d'état.*'

'From whom have you got this?' she cried in wonder. 'You think you have not behaved well? My Prince, were you not young and handsome, I should detest you for your virtues. You push them to the verge of commonplace. And this ingratitude—'

'Understand me, Madame von Rosen,' returned the Prince, flushing a little darker, 'there can be here no talk of gratitude, none of pride. You are here, by what circumstance I know not, but doubtless led by your kindness, mixed up in what regards my family alone. You have no knowledge what my wife, your sovereign, may have suffered; it is not for you—no, nor for me—to judge. I own myself in fault; and were it otherwise, a man were a very empty boaster who should talk of love and start before a small humiliation. It is in all the copybooks that one should die to please his lady-love; and shall a man not go to prison?'

'Love? And what has love to do with being sent to gaol?' exclaimed the Countess, appealing to the walls and roof. 'Heaven knows I think as much of love as any one; my life would prove it; but I admit no love, at least for a man, that is not equally returned. The rest is moonshine.'

'I think of love more absolutely, madam, though I am certain no more tenderly, than a lady to whom I am indebted for such kindnesses,' returned the Prince. 'But this is unavailing. We are not here to hold a court of troubadours.'

'Still,' she replied, 'there is one thing you forget. If she conspires with Gondremark against your liberty, she may conspire with him against your honour also.'

'My honour?' he repeated. 'For a woman, you surprise me. If I have failed to gain her love or play my part of husband, what right is left me? or what honour can remain in such a scene of defeat? No honour that I recognise. I am become a stranger. If my wife no longer loves me, I will go to prison, since she wills it; if she love another, where should I be more in place? or whose fault is it but mine? You speak, Madame von Rosen, like too many women, with a man's tongue. Had I myself fallen into temptation (as, Heaven knows, I might) I should have trembled, but still hoped and asked for her forgiveness; and yet mine had been a treason in the teeth of love. But let me tell you, madam,' he pursued, with rising irritation, 'where a husband by futility, facility, and ill-timed humours has outwearied his wife's patience, I will suffer neither man nor woman to misjudge her. She is free; the man has been found wanting.'

'Because she loves you not?' the Countess cried. 'You know she is incapable of such a feeling.'

'Rather, it was I who was born incapable of inspiring it,' said Otto.

Madame von Rosen broke into sudden laughter. 'Fool,' she cried, 'I am in love with you myself!'

'Ah, madam, you are most compassionate,' the Prince retorted, smiling. 'But this is waste debate. I know my purpose. Perhaps, to equal you in frankness, I know and embrace my advantage. I am not without the spirit of adventure. I am in a false position—so recognised by public acclamation: do you grudge me, then, my issue?'

'If your mind is made up, why should I dissuade you?' said the Countess. 'I own, with a bare face, I am the gainer. Go, you take my heart with you, or more of it than I desire; I shall not sleep at night for thinking of your misery. But do not be afraid; I would not spoil you, you are such a fool and hero.'

'Alas! madam,' cried the Prince, 'and your unlucky money! I did amiss to take it, but you are a wonderful persuader. And I thank God, I can still offer you the fair equivalent.' He took some papers from the chimney. 'Here, madam, are the title-deeds,' he said; 'where I am going, they can certainly be of no use to me, and I have now no other hope of making up to you your kindness. You made the loan without formality, obeying your kind heart. The parts are somewhat changed; the sun of this Prince of Grünewald is upon the point of setting; and I know you better than to doubt you will once more waive ceremony, and accept the best that he can give you. If I may look for any pleasure in the coming time, it will be to remember that the peasant is secure, and my most generous friend no loser.'

'Do you not understand my odious position?' cried the Countess. 'Dear Prince, it is upon your fall that I begin my fortune.'

'It was the more like you to tempt me to resistance,' returned Otto. 'But this cannot alter our relations; and I must, for the last time, lay my commands upon you in the character of Prince.' And with his loftiest dignity, he forced the deeds on her acceptance.

'I hate the very touch of them,' she cried.

There followed upon this a little silence. 'At what time,' resumed Otto, '(if indeed you know) am I to be arrested?'

'Your Highness, when you please!' exclaimed the Countess. 'Or, if you choose to tear that paper, never!'

'I would rather it were done quickly,' said the Prince. 'I shall take but time to leave a letter for the Princess.'

'Well,' said the Countess, 'I have advised you to resist; at the same time, if you intend to be dumb before your shearers, I must say that I ought to set about arranging your arrest. I offered'—she hesitated—'I offered to manage it, intending, my dear friend—intending, upon my soul, to be of use to you. Well, if you will not profit by my goodwill, then be of use to me; and as soon as ever you feel ready, go to the Flying Mercury where we met last night. It will be none the worse for you; and to make it quite plain, it will be better for the rest of us.'

'Dear madam, certainly,' said Otto. 'If I am prepared for the chief evil, I shall not quarrel with details. Go, then, with my best gratitude; and when I have written a few lines of leave-taking, I shall immediately hasten to keep tryst. To-night I shall not meet so dangerous a cavalier,' he added, with a smiling gallantry.

As soon as Madame von Rosen was gone, he made a great call upon his self-command. He was face to face with a miserable passage where, if it were possible, he desired to carry himself with dignity. As to the main fact, he never swerved or faltered; he had come so heart-sick and so cruelly humiliated from his talk with Gotthold, that he embraced the notion of imprisonment with something bordering on relief. Here was, at least, a step which he thought blameless; here was a way out of his troubles. He sat down to write to Seraphina; and his anger blazed. The tale of his forbearances mounted, in his eyes, to something monstrous; still more monstrous, the coldness, egoism, and cruelty that had required and thus requited them. The pen which he had taken shook in his hand. He was amazed to find his resignation fled, but it was gone beyond his recall. In a few white-hot words, he bade adieu, dubbing desperation by the name of love, and calling his wrath forgiveness; then he cast but one look of leave-taking on the place that had been his for so long and was now to be his no longer; and hurried forth—love's prisoner—or pride's.

He took that private passage which he had trodden so often in less momentous hours. The porter let him out; and the bountiful, cold air of the night and the pure glory of the stars received him on the threshold. He looked round him, breathing deep of earth's plain fragrance; he looked up into the great array of heaven, and was quieted. His little turgid life dwindled to its true proportions; and he saw himself (that great flame-hearted martyr!) stand like a speck under the cool cupola of the night. Thus he felt his careless injuries already soothed; the live air of out-of-doors, the quiet of the world, as if by their silent music, sobering and dwarfing his emotions.

'Well, I forgive her,' he said. 'If it be of any use to her, I forgive.'

And with brisk steps he crossed the garden, issued upon the Park, and came to the Flying Mercury. A dark figure moved forward from the shadow of the pedestal.

'I have to ask your pardon, sir,' a voice observed, 'but if I am right in taking you for the Prince, I was given to understand that you would be prepared to meet me.'

'Herr Gordon, I believe?' said Otto.

'Herr Oberst Gordon,' replied that officer. 'This is rather a ticklish business for a man to be embarked in; and to find that all is to go pleasantly is a great relief to me. The carriage is at hand; shall I have the honour of following your Highness?'

'Colonel,' said the Prince, 'I have now come to that happy moment of my life when I have orders to receive but none to give.'

'A most philosophical remark,' returned the Colonel. 'Begad, a very pertinent remark! it might be Plutarch. I am not a drop's blood to your Highness, or indeed to any one in this principality; or else I should dislike my orders. But as it is, and since there is nothing unnatural or unbecoming on my side, and your Highness takes it in good part, I begin to believe we may have a capital time together, sir—a capital time. For a gaoler is only a fellow-captive.'

'May I inquire, Herr Gordon,' asked Otto, 'what led you to accept this dangerous and I would fain hope thankless office?'

'Very natural, I am sure,' replied the officer of fortune. 'My pay is, in the meanwhile, doubled.'

'Well, sir, I will not presume to criticise,' returned the Prince. 'And I perceive the carriage.'

Sure enough, at the intersection of two alleys of the Park, a coach and four, conspicuous by its lanterns, stood in waiting. And a little way off about a score of lancers were drawn up under the shadow of the trees.

CHAPTER XIII
PROVIDENCE VON ROSEN: ACT THE THIRD SHE ENLIGHTENS SERAPHINA

When Madame von Rosen left the Prince, she hurried straight to Colonel Gordon; and not content with directing the arrangements, she had herself accompanied the soldier of fortune to the Flying Mercury. The Colonel gave her his arm, and the talk between this pair of conspirators ran high and lively. The Countess, indeed, was in a whirl of pleasure and excitement; her tongue stumbled upon laughter, her eyes shone, the colour that was usually wanting now perfected her face. It would have taken little more to bring Gordon to her feet—or so, at least, she believed, disdaining the idea.

Hidden among some lilac bushes, she enjoyed the great decorum of the arrest, and heard the dialogue of the two men die away along the path. Soon after, the rolling of a carriage and the beat of hoofs arose in the still air of the night, and passed speedily farther and fainter into silence. The Prince was gone.

Madame von Rosen consulted her watch. She had still, she thought, time enough for the tit-bit of her evening; and hurrying to the palace, winged by the fear of Gondremark's arrival, she sent her name and a pressing request for a reception to the Princess Seraphina. As the Countess von Rosen unqualified, she was sure to be refused; but as an emissary of the Baron's, for so she chose to style herself, she gained immediate entry.

The Princess sat alone at table, making a feint of dining. Her cheeks were mottled, her eyes heavy; she had neither slept nor eaten; even her dress had been neglected. In short, she was out of health, out of looks, out of heart, and hag-ridden by her conscience. The Countess drew a swift comparison, and shone brighter in beauty.

'You come, madam, *de la part de Monsieur le Baron*,' drawled the Princess. 'Be seated! What have you to say?'

'To say?' repeated Madame von Rosen, 'O, much to say! Much to say that I would rather not, and much to leave unsaid that I would rather say. For I am like St. Paul, your Highness, and always wish to do the things I should not. Well! to be categorical—that is the word?—I took the Prince your order. He could not credit his senses. "Ah," he cried "dear Madame von Rosen, it is not possible—it cannot be I must hear it from your lips. My wife is a poor girl misled, she is only silly, she is not cruel." "*Mon Prince*," said I, "a girl—and therefore cruel; youth kills flies."—He had such pain to understand it!'

'Madame von Rosen,' said the Princess, in most steadfast tones, but with a rose of anger in her face, 'who sent you here, and for what purpose? Tell your errand.'

'O, madam, I believe you understand me very well,' returned von Rosen. 'I have not your philosophy. I wear my heart upon my sleeve, excuse the indecency! It is a very little one,' she laughed, 'and I so often change the sleeve!'

'Am I to understand the Prince has been arrested?' asked the Princess, rising.

'While you sat there dining!' cried the Countess, still nonchalantly seated.

'You have discharged your errand,' was the reply; 'I will not detain you.'

'O no, madam,' said the Countess, 'with your permission, I have not yet done. I have borne much this evening in your service. I have suffered. I was made to suffer in your service.' She unfolded her fan as she spoke. Quick as her pulses beat, the fan waved languidly. She betrayed her emotion only by the brightness of her eyes and face, and by the almost insolent triumph with which she looked down upon the Princess. There were old scores of rivalry between them in more than one field; so at least von Rosen felt; and now she was to have her hour of victory in them all.

'You are no servant, Madame von Rosen, of mine,' said Seraphina.

'No, madam, indeed,' returned the Countess; 'but we both serve the same person, as you know—or if you do not, then I have the pleasure of informing you. Your conduct is so light—so light,' she repeated, the fan wavering higher like a butterfly, 'that perhaps you do not truly understand.' The Countess rolled her fan together, laid it in her lap, and rose to a less languorous position. 'Indeed,' she continued, 'I should be sorry to see any young woman in your situation. You began with every advantage—birth, a suitable marriage—quite pretty too—and see what you have come to! My poor girl, to think of it! But there is nothing that does so much harm,' observed the Countess finely, 'as giddiness of mind.' And she once more unfurled the fan, and approvingly fanned herself.

'I will no longer permit you to forget yourself,' cried Seraphina. 'I think you are mad.'

'Not mad,' returned von Rosen. 'Sane enough to know you dare not break with me to-night, and to profit by the knowledge. I left my poor, pretty Prince Charming crying his eyes out for a wooden doll. My heart is soft; I love my pretty Prince; you will never understand it, but I long to give my Prince his doll, dry his poor eyes, and send him off happy. O, you immature fool!' the Countess cried, rising to her feet, and pointing at the Princess the closed fan that now began to tremble in her hand. 'O wooden doll!' she cried, 'have you a heart, or blood, of any nature? This is a man, child—a man who loves you. O, it will not happen twice! it is not common; beautiful and clever women look in vain for it. And you, you pitiful schoolgirl, tread this jewel under foot! you, stupid with your vanity! Before you try to govern kingdoms, you should first be able to behave yourself at home; home is the woman's kingdom.' She paused and laughed a little, strangely to hear and look upon. 'I will tell you one of the things,' she said, 'that were to stay unspoken. Von Rosen is a better women than you, my Princess, though you will never have the pain of understanding it; and when I took the Prince your order, and looked upon his face, my soul was melted—O, I am frank—here, within my arms, I offered him repose!' She advanced a step superbly as she spoke, with outstretched arms; and Seraphina shrank. 'Do not be alarmed!' the Countess cried; 'I am not offering that hermitage to you; in all the world there is but one who wants to, and him you have dismissed! "If it will give her pleasure I should wear the martyr's crown," he cried, "I will embrace the thorns." I tell you—I am quite frank—I put the order in his power and begged him to resist. You, who have betrayed your husband, may betray me to Gondremark; my Prince would betray no one. Understand it plainly,' she cried, ''tis of his pure forbearance that you sit there; he had the power—I gave it him—to change the parts; and he refused, and went to prison in your place.'

The Princess spoke with some distress. 'Your violence shocks me and pains me,' she began, 'but I cannot be angry with what at least does honour to the mistaken kindness of your heart: it was right for me to know this. I will condescend to tell you. It was with deep regret that I was driven to this step. I admire in many ways the Prince—I admit his amiability. It was our great misfortune, it was perhaps somewhat of my fault, that we were so unsuited to each other; but I have a regard, a sincere regard, for all his qualities. As a private person I should think as you do. It is difficult, I know, to make allowances for state considerations. I have only with deep reluctance obeyed the call of a superior duty; and so soon as I dare do it for the safety of the state, I promise you the Prince shall be released. Many in my situation would have resented your freedoms. I am not'—and she looked for a moment rather piteously upon the Countess—'I am not altogether so inhuman as you think.'

'And you can put these troubles of the state,' the Countess cried, 'to weigh with a man's love?'

'Madame von Rosen, these troubles are affairs of life and death to many; to the Prince, and perhaps even to yourself, among the number,' replied the Princess, with dignity. 'I have learned, madam, although still so young, in a hard school, that my own feelings must everywhere come last.'

'O callow innocence!' exclaimed the other. 'Is it possible you do not know, or do not suspect, the intrigue in which you move? I find it in my heart to pity you! We are both women after all—poor girl, poor girl!—and who is born a woman is born a fool. And though I hate all women—come, for the common folly, I forgive you. Your Highness'—she dropped a deep stage curtsey and resumed her fan—'I am going to insult you, to betray one who is called my lover, and if it pleases you to use the power I now put unreservedly into your hands, to ruin my dear self. O what a French comedy! You betray, I betray, they betray. It is now my cue. The letter, yes. Behold the letter, madam, its seal unbroken as I found it by my bed this morning; for I was out of humour, and I get many, too many, of these favours. For your own sake, for the sake of my Prince Charming, for the sake of this great principality that sits so heavy on your conscience, open it and read!'

'Am I to understand,' inquired the Princess, 'that this letter in any way regards me?'

'You see I have not opened it,' replied von Rosen; 'but 'tis mine, and I beg you to experiment.'

'I cannot look at it till you have,' returned Seraphina, very seriously. 'There may be matter there not meant for me to see; it is a private letter.'

The Countess tore it open, glanced it through, and tossed it back; and the Princess, taking up the sheet, recognised the hand of Gondremark, and read with a sickening shock the following lines:—

> 'Dearest Anna, come at once. Ratafia has done the deed, her husband is to be packed to prison. This puts the minx entirely in my power; *le tour est joué*; she will now go steady in harness, or I will know the reason why. Come.
>
> HEINRICH.'

'Command yourself, madam,' said the Countess, watching with some alarm the white face of Seraphina. 'It is in vain for you to fight with Gondremark; he has more strings than mere court favour, and could bring you down to-morrow with a word. I would not have betrayed him otherwise; but Heinrich is a man, and plays with all of you like marionnettes. And now at least you see for what you sacrificed my Prince. Madam, will you take some wine? I have been cruel.'

'Not cruel, madam—salutary,' said Seraphina, with a phantom smile. 'No, I thank you, I require no attentions. The first surprise affected me: will you give me time a little? I must think.'

She took her head between her hands, and contemplated for a while the hurricane confusion of her thoughts.

'This information reaches me,' she said, 'when I have need of it. I would not do as you have done, but yet I thank you. I have been much deceived in Baron Gondremark.'

'O, madam, leave Gondremark, and think upon the Prince!' cried von Rosen.

'You speak once more as a private person,' said the Princess; 'nor do I blame you. But my own thoughts are more distracted. However, as I believe you are truly a friend to my—to the—as I believe,' she said, 'you are a friend to Otto, I shall put the order for his release into your hands this moment. Give me the ink-dish. There!' And she wrote hastily, steadying her arm upon the table, for she trembled like a reed. 'Remember; madam,' she resumed, handing her the order, 'this must not be used nor spoken of at present; till I have seen the Baron, any hurried step—I lose myself in thinking. The suddenness has shaken me.'

'I promise you I will not use it,' said the Countess, 'till you give me leave, although I wish the Prince could be informed of it, to comfort his poor heart. And O, I had forgotten, he has left a letter. Suffer me, madam, I will bring it you. This is the door, I think?' And she sought to open it.

'The bolt is pushed,' said Seraphina, flushing.

'O! O!' cried the Countess.

A silence fell between them.

'I will get it for myself,' said Seraphina; 'and in the meanwhile I beg you to leave me. I thank you, I am sure, but I shall be obliged if you will leave me.'

The Countess deeply curtseyed, and withdrew.

CHAPTER XIV
RELATES THE CAUSE AND OUTBREAK OF
THE REVOLUTION

Brave as she was, and brave by intellect, the Princess, when first she was alone, clung to the table for support. The four corners of her universe had fallen. She had never liked nor trusted Gondremark completely; she had still held it possible to find him false to friendship; but from that to finding him devoid of all those public virtues for which she had honoured him, a mere commonplace intriguer, using her for his own ends, the step was wide and the descent giddy. Light and darkness succeeded each other in her brain; now she believed, and now she could not. She turned, blindly groping for the note. But von Rosen, who had not forgotten to take the warrant from the Prince, had remembered to recover her note from the Princess: von Rosen was an old campaigner, whose most violent emotion aroused rather than clouded the vigour of her reason.

The thought recalled to Seraphina the remembrance of the other letter— Otto's. She rose and went speedily, her brain still wheeling, and burst into the Prince's armoury. The old chamberlain was there in waiting; and the sight of another face, prying (or so she felt) on her distress, struck Seraphina into childish anger.

'Go!' she cried; and then, when the old man was already half-way to the door, 'Stay!' she added. 'As soon as Baron Gondremark arrives, let him attend me here.'

'It shall be so directed,' said the chamberlain.

'There was a letter . . . ' she began, and paused.

'Her Highness,' said the chamberlain, 'will, find a letter on the table. I had received no orders, or her Highness had been spared this trouble.'

'No, no, no,' she cried. 'I thank you. I desire to be alone.'

And then, when he was gone, she leaped upon the letter. Her mind was still obscured; like the moon upon a night of clouds and wind, her reason shone and was darkened, and she read the words by flashes.

> 'Seraphina,' the Prince wrote, 'I will write no syllable of reproach. I have seen your order, and I go. What else is left me? I have wasted my love, and have no more. To say that I forgive you is not needful; at least, we are now

separate for ever; by your own act, you free me from my willing bondage: I go free to prison. This is the last that you will hear of me in love or anger. I have gone out of your life; you may breathe easy; you have now rid yourself of the husband who allowed you to desert him, of the Prince who gave you his rights, and of the married lover who made it his pride to defend you in your absence. How you have requited him, your own heart more loudly tells you than my words. There is a day coming when your vain dreams will roll away like clouds, and you will find yourself alone. Then you will remember

OTTO.'

She read with a great horror on her mind; that day, of which he wrote, was come. She was alone; she had been false, she had been cruel; remorse rolled in upon her; and then with a more piercing note, vanity bounded on the stage of consciousness. She a dupe! she helpless! she to have betrayed herself in seeking to betray her husband! she to have lived these years upon flattery, grossly swallowing the bolus, like a clown with sharpers! she— Seraphina! Her swift mind drank the consequences; she foresaw the coming fall, her public shame; she saw the odium, disgrace, and folly of her story flaunt through Europe. She recalled the scandal she had so royally braved; and alas! she had now no courage to confront it with. To be thought the mistress of that man: perhaps for that. . . . She closed her eyes on agonising vistas. Swift as thought she had snatched a bright dagger from the weapons that shone along the wall. Ay, she would escape. From that world-wide theatre of nodding heads and buzzing whisperers, in which she now beheld herself unpitiably martyred, one door stood open. At any cost, through any stress of suffering, that greasy laughter should be stifled. She closed her eyes, breathed a wordless prayer, and pressed the weapon to her bosom.

At the astonishing sharpness of the prick, she gave a cry and awoke to a sense of undeserved escape. A little ruby spot of blood was the reward of that great act of desperation; but the pain had braced her like a tonic, and her whole design of suicide had passed away.

At the same instant regular feet drew near along the gallery, and she knew the tread of the big Baron, so often gladly welcome, and even now rallying her spirits like a call to battle. She concealed the dagger in the folds of her skirt; and drawing her stature up, she stood firm-footed, radiant with anger, waiting for the foe.

The Baron was announced, and entered. To him, Seraphina was a hated task: like the schoolboy with his Virgil, he had neither will nor leisure to remark her beauties; but when he now beheld her standing illuminated by her passion, new feelings flashed upon him, a frank admiration, a brief sparkle of desire. He noted both with joy; they were means. 'If I have to play the lover,' thought he, for that was his constant preoccupation, 'I believe I can put soul into it.' Meanwhile, with his usual ponderous grace, he bent before the lady.

'I propose,' she said in a strange voice, not known to her till then, 'that we release the Prince and do not prosecute the war.'

'Ah, madam,' he replied, ''tis as I knew it would be! Your heart, I knew, would wound you when we came to this distasteful but most necessary step. Ah, madam, believe me, I am not unworthy to be your ally; I know you have qualities to which I am a stranger, and count them the best weapons in the armoury of our alliance:—the girl in the queen—pity, love, tenderness, laughter; the smile that can reward. I can only command; I am the frowner. But you! And you have the fortitude to command these comely weaknesses, to tread them down at the call of reason. How often have I not admired it even to yourself! Ay, even to yourself,' he added tenderly, dwelling, it seemed, in memory on hours of more private admiration. 'But now, madam—'

'But now, Herr von Gondremark, the time for these declarations has gone by,' she cried. 'Are you true to me? are you false? Look in your heart and answer: it is your heart I want to know.'

'It has come,' thought Gondremark. 'You, madam!' he cried, starting back—with fear, you would have said, and yet a timid joy. 'You! yourself, you bid me look into my heart?'

'Do you suppose I fear?' she cried, and looked at him with such a heightened colour, such bright eyes, and a smile of so abstruse a meaning, that the Baron discarded his last doubt.

'Ah, madam!' he cried, plumping on his knees. 'Seraphina! Do you permit me? have you divined my secret? It is true—I put my life with joy into your power—I love you, love with ardour, as an equal, as a mistress, as a brother-in-arms, as an adored, desired, sweet-hearted woman. O Bride!' he cried, waxing dithyrambic, 'bride of my reason and my senses, have pity, have pity on my love!'

She heard him with wonder, rage, and then contempt. His words offended her to sickness; his appearance, as he grovelled bulkily upon the floor, moved her to such laughter as we laugh in nightmares.

'O shame!' she cried. 'Absurd and odious! What would the Countess say?'

That great Baron Gondremark, the excellent politician, remained for some little time upon his knees in a frame of mind which perhaps we are allowed to pity. His vanity, within his iron bosom, bled and raved. If he could have blotted all, if he could have withdrawn part, if he had not called her bride— with a roaring in his ears, he thus regretfully reviewed his declaration. He got to his feet tottering; and then, in that first moment when a dumb agony finds a vent in words, and the tongue betrays the inmost and worst of a man, he permitted himself a retort which, for six weeks to follow, he was to repent at leisure.

'Ah,' said he, 'the Countess? Now I perceive the reason of your Highness's disorder.'

The lackey-like insolence of the words was driven home by a more insolent manner. There fell upon Seraphina one of those storm-clouds which had already blackened upon her reason; she heard herself cry out; and when the cloud dispersed, flung the blood-stained dagger on the floor, and saw Gondremark reeling back with open mouth and clapping his hand upon the wound. The next moment, with oaths that she had never heard, he leaped at her in savage passion; clutched her as she recoiled; and in the very act, stumbled and drooped. She had scarce time to fear his murderous onslaught ere he fell before her feet.

He rose upon one elbow; she still staring upon him, white with horror.

'Anna!' he cried, 'Anna! Help!'

And then his utterance failed him, and he fell back, to all appearance dead.

Seraphina ran to and fro in the room; she wrung her hands and cried aloud; within she was all one uproar of terror, and conscious of no articulate wish but to awake.

There came a knocking at the door; and she sprang to it and held it, panting like a beast, and with the strength of madness in her arms, till she had pushed the bolt. At this success a certain calm fell upon her reason. She went back and looked upon her victim, the knocking growing louder. O yes, he was dead. She had killed him. He had called upon von Rosen with his latest breath; ah! who would call on Seraphina? She had killed him. She, whose irresolute hand could scarce prick blood from her own bosom, had found strength to cast down that great colossus at a blow.

All this while the knocking was growing more uproarious and more unlike the staid career of life in such a palace. Scandal was at the door, with what a fatal following she dreaded to conceive; and at the same time among the voices that now began to summon her by name, she recognised the Chancellor's. He or another, somebody must be the first.

'Is Herr von Greisengesang without?' she called.

'Your Highness—yes!' the old gentleman answered. 'We have heard cries, a fall. Is anything amiss?'

'Nothing,' replied Seraphina 'I desire to speak with you. Send off the rest.' She panted between each phrase; but her mind was clear. She let the looped curtain down upon both sides before she drew the bolt; and, thus secure from any sudden eyeshot from without, admitted the obsequious Chancellor, and again made fast the door.

Greisengesang clumsily revolved among the wings of the curtain, so that she was clear of it as soon as he.

'My God!' he cried 'The Baron!'

'I have killed him,' she said. 'O, killed him!'

'Dear me,' said the old gentleman, 'this is most unprecedented. Lovers' quarrels,' he added ruefully, 'redintegratio—' and then paused. 'But, my dear madam,' he broke out again, 'in the name of all that is practical, what are we to do? This is exceedingly grave; morally, madam, it is appalling. I take the liberty, your Highness, for one moment, of addressing you as a daughter, a loved although respected daughter; and I must say that I cannot conceal from you that this is morally most questionable. And, O dear me, we have a dead body!'

She had watched him closely; hope fell to contempt; she drew away her skirts from his weakness, and, in the act, her own strength returned to her.

'See if he be dead,' she said; not one word of explanation or defence; she had scorned to justify herself before so poor a creature: 'See if he be dead' was all.

With the greatest compunction, the Chancellor drew near; and as he did so the wounded Baron rolled his eyes.

'He lives,' cried the old courtier, turning effusively to Seraphina. 'Madam, he still lives.'

'Help him, then,' returned the Princess, standing fixed. 'Bind up his wound.'

'Madam, I have no means,' protested the Chancellor.

'Can you not take your handkerchief, your neck-cloth, anything?' she cried; and at the same moment, from her light muslin gown she rent off a flounce and tossed it on the floor. 'Take that,' she said, and for the first time directly faced Greisengesang.

But the Chancellor held up his hands and turned away his head in agony. The grasp of the falling Baron had torn down the dainty fabric of the bodice; and—'O Highness!' cried Greisengesang, appalled, 'the terrible disorder of your toilette!'

'Take up that flounce,' she said; 'the man may die.'

Greisengesang turned in a flutter to the Baron, and attempted some innocent and bungling measures. 'He still breathes,' he kept saying. 'All is not yet over; he is not yet gone.'

'And now,' said she 'if that is all you can do, begone and get some porters; he must instantly go home.'

'Madam,' cried the Chancellor, 'if this most melancholy sight were seen in town—O dear, the State would fall!' he piped.

'There is a litter in the Palace,' she replied. 'It is your part to see him safe. I lay commands upon you. On your life it stands.'

'I see it, dear Highness,' he jerked. 'Clearly I see it. But how? what men? The Prince's servants—yes. They had a personal affection. They will be true, if any.'

'O, not them!' she cried. 'Take Sabra, my own man.'

'Sabra! The grand-mason?' returned the Chancellor, aghast. 'If he but saw this, he would sound the tocsin—we should all be butchered.'

She measured the depth of her abasement steadily. 'Take whom you must,' she said, 'and bring the litter here.'

Once she was alone she ran to the Baron, and with a sickening heart sought to allay the flux of blood. The touch of the skin of that great charlatan revolted her to the toes; the wound, in her ignorant eyes, looked deathly; yet she contended with her shuddering, and, with more skill at least than the Chancellor's, staunched the welling injury. An eye unprejudiced with hate would have admired the Baron in his swoon; he looked so great and shapely; it was so powerful a machine that lay arrested; and his features, cleared for the moment both of temper and dissimulation, were seen to be so purely modelled. But it was not thus with Seraphina. Her victim, as he lay outspread, twitching a little, his big chest unbared, fixed her with his ugliness; and her mind flitted for a glimpse to Otto.

Rumours began to sound about the Palace of feet running and of voices raised; the echoes of the great arched staircase were voluble of some confusion; and then the gallery jarred with a quick and heavy tramp. It was the Chancellor, followed by four of Otto's valets and a litter. The servants, when they were admitted, stared at the dishevelled Princess and the wounded man; speech was denied them, but their thoughts were riddled with profanity. Gondremark was bundled in; the curtains of the litter were lowered; the bearers carried it forth, and the Chancellor followed behind with a white face.

Seraphina ran to the window. Pressing her face upon the pane, she could see the terrace, where the lights contended; thence, the avenue of lamps that joined the Palace and town; and overhead the hollow night and the larger stars. Presently the small procession issued from the Palace, crossed the parade, and began to thread the glittering alley: the swinging couch with its four porters, the much-pondering Chancellor behind. She watched them dwindle with strange thoughts: her eyes fixed upon the scene, her mind still glancing right and left on the overthrow of her life and hopes. There was no one left in whom she might confide; none whose hand was friendly, or on whom she dared to reckon for the barest loyalty. With the fall of Gondremark, her party, her brief popularity, had fallen. So she sat crouched upon the window-seat, her brow to the cool pane; her dress in tatters, barely shielding her; her mind revolving bitter thoughts.

Meanwhile, consequences were fast mounting; and in the deceptive quiet of the night, downfall and red revolt were brewing. The litter had passed forth between the iron gates and entered on the streets of the town. By what flying panic, by what thrill of air communicated, who shall say? but the passing bustle in the Palace had already reached and re-echoed in the region of the burghers. Rumour, with her loud whisper, hissed about the town; men left their homes without knowing why; knots formed along the boulevard; under the rare lamps and the great limes the crowd grew blacker.

And now through the midst of that expectant company, the unusual sight of a closed litter was observed approaching, and trotting hard behind it that great dignitary Cancellarius Greisengesang. Silence looked on as it went by; and as soon as it was passed, the whispering seethed over like a boiling pot. The knots were sundered; and gradually, one following another, the whole mob began to form into a procession and escort the curtained litter. Soon spokesmen, a little bolder than their mates, began to ply the Chancellor with questions. Never had he more need of that great art of falsehood, by whose exercise he had so richly lived. And yet now he stumbled, the master passion, fear, betraying him. He was pressed; he became incoherent; and then from the jolting litter came a groan. In the instant hubbub and the gathering of the crowd as to a natural signal, the clear-eyed quavering Chancellor heard the catch of the clock before it strikes the hour of doom; and for ten seconds he forgot himself. This shall atone for many sins. He plucked a bearer by the sleeve. 'Bid the Princess flee. All is lost,' he whispered. And the next moment he was babbling for his life among the multitude.

Five minutes later the wild-eyed servant burst into the armoury. 'All is lost!' he cried. 'The Chancellor bids you flee.' And at the same time, looking through the window, Seraphina saw the black rush of the populace begin to invade the lamplit avenue.

'Thank you, Georg,' she said. 'I thank you. Go.' And as the man still lingered, 'I bid you go,' she added. 'Save yourself.'

Down by the private passage, and just some two hours later, Amalia Seraphina, the last Princess, followed Otto Johann Friedrich, the last Prince of Grünewald.

BOOK III
FORTUNATE MISFORTUNE

CHAPTER I
PRINCESS CINDERELLA

The porter, drawn by the growing turmoil, had vanished from the postern, and the door stood open on the darkness of the night. As Seraphina fled up the terraces, the cries and loud footing of the mob drew nearer the doomed palace; the rush was like the rush of cavalry; the sound of shattering lamps tingled above the rest; and, overtowering all, she heard her own name bandied among the shouters. A bugle sounded at the door of the guard-room; one gun was fired; and then with the yell of hundreds, Mittwalden Palace was carried at a rush.

Sped by these dire sounds and voices, the Princess scaled the long garden, skimming like a bird the starlit stairways; crossed the Park, which was in that place narrow; and plunged upon the farther side into the rude shelter of the forest. So, at a bound, she left the discretion and the cheerful lamps of Palace evenings; ceased utterly to be a sovereign lady; and, falling from the whole height of civilisation, ran forth into the woods, a ragged Cinderella.

She went direct before her through an open tract of the forest, full of brush and birches, and where the starlight guided her; and, beyond that again, must thread the columned blackness of a pine grove joining overhead the thatch of its long branches. At that hour the place was breathless; a horror of night like a presence occupied that dungeon of the wood; and she went groping, knocking against the boles—her ear, betweenwhiles, strained to aching and yet unrewarded.

But the slope of the ground was upward, and encouraged her; and presently she issued on a rocky hill that stood forth above the sea of forest. All around were other hill-tops, big and little; sable vales of forest between; overhead the open heaven and the brilliancy of countless stars; and along the western sky the dim forms of mountains. The glory of the great night laid hold upon her; her eyes shone with stars; she dipped her sight into the coolness and brightness of the sky, as she might have dipped her wrist into a spring; and her heart, at that ethereal shock, began to move more soberly. The sun that sails overhead, ploughing into gold the fields of daylight azure and uttering the signal to man's myriads, has no word apart for man the individual; and the moon, like a violin, only praises and laments our private destiny. The stars alone, cheerful whisperers, confer quietly with each of us like friends; they give ear to our sorrows smilingly, like wise old men, rich in tolerance; and by their double scale, so small to the eye, so vast to the imagination, they keep before the mind the double character of man's nature and fate.

There sat the Princess, beautifully looking upon beauty, in council with these glad advisers. Bright like pictures, clear like a voice in the porches of her ear, memory re-enacted the tumult of the evening: the Countess and the dancing fan, the big Baron on his knees, the blood on the polished floor, the knocking, the swing of the litter down the avenue of lamps, the messenger, the cries of the charging mob; and yet all were far away and phantasmal, and she was still healingly conscious of the peace and glory of the night. She looked towards Mittwalden; and above the hill-top, which already hid it from her view, a throbbing redness hinted of fire. Better so: better so, that she should fall with tragic greatness, lit by a blazing palace! She felt not a trace of pity for Gondremark or of concern for Grünewald: that period of her life was closed for ever, a wrench of wounded vanity alone surviving. She had but one clear idea: to flee;—and another, obscure and half-rejected, although still obeyed: to flee in the direction of the Felsenburg. She had a duty to perform, she must free Otto—so her mind said, very coldly; but her heart embraced the notion of that duty even with ardour, and her hands began to yearn for the grasp of kindness.

She rose, with a start of recollection, and plunged down the slope into the covert. The woods received and closed upon her. Once more, she wandered and hasted in a blot, uncheered, unpiloted. Here and there, indeed, through rents in the wood-roof, a glimmer attracted her; here and there a tree stood out among its neighbours by some force of outline; here and there a brushing among the leaves, a notable blackness, a dim shine, relieved, only to exaggerate, the solid oppression of the night and silence. And betweenwhiles, the unfeatured darkness would redouble and the whole ear of night appear to be gloating on her steps. Now she would stand still, and the silence, would grow and grow, till it weighed upon her breathing; and then she would address herself again to run, stumbling, falling, and still hurrying the more. And presently the whole wood rocked and began to run along with her. The noise of her own mad passage through the silence spread and echoed, and filled the night with terror. Panic hunted her: Panic from the trees reached forth with clutching branches; the darkness was lit up and peopled with strange forms and faces. She strangled and fled before her fears. And yet in the last fortress, reason, blown upon by these gusts of terror, still shone with a troubled light. She knew, yet could not act upon her knowledge; she knew that she must stop, and yet she still ran.

She was already near madness, when she broke suddenly into a narrow clearing. At the same time the din grew louder, and she became conscious of vague forms and fields of whiteness. And with that the earth gave way;

she fell and found her feet again with an incredible shock to her senses, and her mind was swallowed up.

When she came again to herself, she was standing to the mid-leg in an icy eddy of a brook, and leaning with one hand on the rock from which it poured. The spray had wet her hair. She saw the white cascade, the stars wavering in the shaken pool, foam flitting, and high overhead the tall pines on either hand serenely drinking starshine; and in the sudden quiet of her spirit she heard with joy the firm plunge of the cataract in the pool. She scrambled forth dripping. In the face of her proved weakness, to adventure again upon the horror of blackness in the groves were a suicide of life or reason. But here, in the alley of the brook, with the kind stars above her, and the moon presently swimming into sight, she could await the coming of day without alarm.

This lane of pine-trees ran very rapidly down-hill and wound among the woods; but it was a wider thoroughfare than the brook needed, and here and there were little dimpling lawns and coves of the forest, where the starshine slumbered. Such a lawn she paced, taking patience bravely; and now she looked up the hill and saw the brook coming down to her in a series of cascades; and now approached the margin, where it welled among the rushes silently; and now gazed at the great company of heaven with an enduring wonder. The early evening had fallen chill, but the night was now temperate; out of the recesses of the wood there came mild airs as from a deep and peaceful breathing; and the dew was heavy on the grass and the tight-shut daisies. This was the girl's first night under the naked heaven; and now that her fears were overpast, she was touched to the soul by its serene amenity and peace. Kindly the host of heaven blinked down upon that wandering Princess; and the honest brook had no words but to encourage her.

At last she began to be aware of a wonderful revolution, compared to which the fire of Mittwalden Palace was but the crack and flash of a percussion-cap. The countenance with which the pines regarded her began insensibly to change; the grass too, short as it was, and the whole winding staircase of the brook's course, began to wear a solemn freshness of appearance. And this slow transfiguration reached her heart, and played upon it, and transpierced it with a serious thrill. She looked all about; the whole face of nature looked back, brimful of meaning, finger on lip, leaking its glad secret. She looked up. Heaven was almost emptied of stars. Such as still lingered shone with a changed and waning brightness, and began to faint in their stations. And the colour of the sky itself was the most wonderful; for the rich blue of the night had now melted and softened and brightened; and there had succeeded in its place a hue that has no name, and that is never seen but as the herald of morning. 'O!' she cried, joy catching at her voice, 'O! it is the dawn!'

In a breath she passed over the brook, and looped up her skirts and fairly ran in the dim alleys. As she ran, her ears were aware of many pipings, more beautiful than music; in the small dish-shaped houses in the fork of giant arms, where they had lain all night, lover by lover, warmly pressed, the bright-eyed, big-hearted singers began to awaken for the day. Her heart melted and flowed forth to them in kindness. And they, from their small and high perches in the clerestories of the wood cathedral, peered down sidelong at the ragged Princess as she flitted below them on the carpet of the moss and tassel.

Soon she had struggled to a certain hill-top, and saw far before her the silent inflooding of the day. Out of the East it welled and whitened; the darkness trembled into light; and the stars were extinguished like the street-lamps of a human city. The whiteness brightened into silver, the silver warmed into gold, the gold kindled into pure and living fire; and the face of the East was barred with elemental scarlet. The day drew its first long breath, steady and chill; and for leagues around the woods sighed and shivered. And then, at one bound, the sun had floated up; and her startled eyes received day's first arrow, and quailed under the buffet. On every side, the shadows leaped from their ambush and fell prone. The day was come, plain and garish; and up the steep and solitary eastern heaven, the sun, victorious over his competitors, continued slowly and royally to mount.

Seraphina drooped for a little, leaning on a pine, the shrill joy of the woodlands mocking her. The shelter of the night, the thrilling and joyous changes of the dawn, were over; and now, in the hot eye of the day, she turned uneasily and looked sighingly about her. Some way off among the lower woods, a pillar of smoke was mounting and melting in the gold and blue. There, surely enough, were human folk, the hearth-surrounders. Man's fingers had laid the twigs; it was man's breath that had quickened and encouraged the baby flames; and now, as the fire caught, it would be playing ruddily on the face of its creator. At the thought, she felt a-cold and little and lost in that great out-of-doors. The electric shock of the young sun-beams and the unhuman beauty of the woods began to irk and daunt her. The covert of the house, the decent privacy of rooms, the swept and regulated fire, all that denotes or beautifies the home life of man, began to draw her as with cords. The pillar of smoke was now risen into some stream of moving air; it began to lean out sideways in a pennon; and thereupon, as though the change had been a summons, Seraphina plunged once more into the labyrinth of the wood.

She left day upon the high ground. In the lower groves there still lingered the blue early twilight and the seizing freshness of the dew. But here and there, above this field of shadow, the head of a great outspread pine was already glorious with day; and here and there, through the breaches of the hills, the sun-beams made a great and luminous entry. Here Seraphina hastened along forest paths. She had lost sight of the pilot smoke, which blew another way, and conducted herself in that great wilderness by the direction of the sun. But presently fresh signs bespoke the neighbourhood of man; felled trunks, white slivers from the axe, bundles of green boughs, and stacks of firewood. These guided her forward; until she came forth at last upon the clearing whence the smoke arose. A hut stood in the clear shadow, hard by a brook which made a series of inconsiderable falls; and on the threshold the Princess saw a sun-burnt and hard-featured woodman, standing with his hands behind his back and gazing skyward.

She went to him directly: a beautiful, bright-eyed, and haggard vision; splendidly arrayed and pitifully tattered; the diamond ear-drops still glittering in her ears; and with the movement of her coming, one small breast showing and hiding among the ragged covert of the laces. At that ambiguous hour, and coming as she did from the great silence of the forest, the man drew back from the Princess as from something elfin.

'I am cold,' she said, 'and weary. Let me rest beside your fire.'

The woodman was visibly commoved, but answered nothing.

'I will pay,' she said, and then repented of the words, catching perhaps a spark of terror from his frightened eyes. But, as usual, her courage rekindled brighter for the check. She put him from the door and entered; and he followed her in superstitious wonder.

Within, the hut was rough and dark; but on the stone that served as hearth, twigs and a few dry branches burned with the brisk sounds and all the variable beauty of fire. The very sight of it composed her; she crouched hard by on the earth floor and shivered in the glow, and looked upon the eating blaze with admiration. The woodman was still staring at his guest: at the wreck of the rich dress, the bare arms, the bedraggled laces and the gems. He found no word to utter.

'Give me food,' said she,—'here, by the fire.'

He set down a pitcher of coarse wine, bread, a piece of cheese, and a handful of raw onions. The bread was hard and sour, the cheese like leather; even the onion, which ranks with the truffle and the nectarine in the chief place of honour of earth's fruits, is not perhaps a dish for princesses when raw. But she ate, if not with appetite, with courage; and when she had eaten, did not disdain the pitcher. In all her life before, she had not tasted of gross food nor drunk after another; but a brave woman far more readily accepts a change of circumstances than the bravest man. All that while, the woodman continued to observe her furtively, many low thoughts of fear and greed contending in his eyes. She read them clearly, and she knew she must begone.

Presently she arose and offered him a florin.

'Will that repay you?' she asked.

But here the man found his tongue. 'I must have more than that,' said he.

'It is all I have to give you,' she returned, and passed him by serenely.

Yet her heart trembled, for she saw his hand stretched forth as if to arrest her, and his unsteady eyes wandering to his axe. A beaten path led westward from the clearing, and she swiftly followed it. She did not glance behind her. But as soon as the least turning of the path had concealed her from the woodman's eyes, she slipped among the trees and ran till she deemed herself in safety.

By this time the strong sunshine pierced in a thousand places the pine-thatch of the forest, fired the red boles, irradiated the cool aisles of shadow, and burned in jewels on the grass. The gum of these trees was dearer to the senses than the gums of Araby; each pine, in the lusty morning sunlight, burned its own wood-incense; and now and then a breeze would rise and toss these rooted censers, and send shade and sun-gem flitting, swift as swallows, thick as bees; and wake a brushing bustle of sounds that murmured and went by.

On she passed, and up and down, in sun and shadow; now aloft on the bare ridge among the rocks and birches, with the lizards and the snakes; and anon in the deep grove among sunless pillars. Now she followed wandering wood-paths, in the maze of valleys; and again, from a hill-top, beheld the distant mountains and the great birds circling under the sky. She would see afar off a nestling hamlet, and go round to avoid it. Below, she traced the course of the foam of mountain torrents. Nearer hand, she saw where the tender springs welled up in silence, or oozed in green moss; or in the more favoured hollows a whole family of infant rivers would combine, and tinkle in the stones, and lie in pools to be a bathing-place for sparrows, or fall from the sheer rock in rods of crystal. Upon all these things, as she still sped along in the bright air, she looked with a rapture of surprise and a joyful fainting of the heart; they seemed so novel, they touched so strangely home, they were so hued and scented, they were so beset and canopied by the dome of the blue air of heaven.

At length, when she was well weary, she came upon a wide and shallow pool. Stones stood in it, like islands; bulrushes fringed the coast; the floor was paved with the pine needles; and the pines themselves, whose roots made promontories, looked down silently on their green images. She crept to the margin and beheld herself with wonder, a hollow and bright-eyed phantom, in the ruins of her palace robe. The breeze now shook her image; now it would be marred with flies; and at that she smiled; and from the fading circles, her counterpart smiled back to her and looked kind. She sat long in the warm sun, and pitied her bare arms that were all bruised and marred with falling, and marvelled to see that she was dirty, and could not grow to believe that she had gone so long in such a strange disorder.

Then, with a sigh, she addressed herself to make a toilette by that forest mirror, washed herself pure from all the stains of her adventure, took off her jewels and wrapped them in her handkerchief, re-arranged the tatters of her dress, and took down the folds of her hair. She shook it round her face, and the pool repeated her thus veiled. Her hair had smelt like violets, she remembered Otto saying; and so now she tried to smell it, and then shook her head, and laughed a little, sadly, to herself.

The laugh was returned upon her in a childish echo.

She looked up; and lo! two children looking on,—a small girl and a yet smaller boy, standing, like playthings, by the pool, below a spreading pine. Seraphina was not fond of children, and now she was startled to the heart.

'Who are you?' she cried hoarsely.

The mites huddled together and drew back; and Seraphina's heart reproached her that she should have frightened things so quaint and little, and yet alive with senses. She thought upon the birds and looked again at her two visitors; so little larger and so far more innocent. On their clear faces, as in a pool, she saw the reflection of their fears. With gracious purpose she arose.

'Come,' she said, 'do not be afraid of me,' and took a step towards them.

But alas! at the first moment, the two poor babes in the wood turned and ran helter-skelter from the Princess.

The most desolate pang was struck into the girl's heart. Here she was, twenty-two—soon twenty-three—and not a creature loved her; none but Otto; and would even he forgive? If she began weeping in these woods alone, it would mean death or madness. Hastily she trod the thoughts out like a burning paper; hastily rolled up her locks, and with terror dogging her, and her whole bosom sick with grief, resumed her journey.

Past ten in the forenoon, she struck a high-road, marching in that place uphill between two stately groves, a river of sunlight; and here, dead weary, careless of consequences, and taking some courage from the human and civilised neighbourhood of the road, she stretched herself on the green margin in the shadow of a tree. Sleep closed on her, at first with a horror of fainting, but when she ceased to struggle, kindly embracing her. So she was taken home for a little, from all her toils and sorrows, to her Father's arms. And there in the meanwhile her body lay exposed by the highwayside, in tattered finery; and on either hand from the woods the birds came flying by and calling upon others, and debated in their own tongue this strange appearance.

The sun pursued his journey; the shadow flitted from her feet, shrank higher and higher, and was upon the point of leaving her altogether, when the rumble of a coach was signalled to and fro by the birds. The road in that part was very steep; the rumble drew near with great deliberation; and ten minutes passed before a gentleman appeared, walking with a sober elderly gait upon the grassy margin of the highway, and looking pleasantly around him as he walked. From time to time he paused, took out his note-book and made an entry with a pencil; and any spy who had been near enough would have heard him mumbling words as though he were a poet testing verses. The voice of the wheels was still faint, and it was plain the traveller had far outstripped his carriage.

He had drawn very near to where the Princess lay asleep, before his eye alighted on her; but when it did he started, pocketed his note-book, and approached. There was a milestone close to where she lay; and he sat down on that and coolly studied her. She lay upon one side, all curled and sunken, her brow on one bare arm, the other stretched out, limp and dimpled. Her young body, like a thing thrown down, had scarce a mark of life. Her breathing stirred her not. The deadliest fatigue was thus confessed in every language of the sleeping flesh. The traveller smiled grimly. As though he had looked upon a statue, he made a grudging inventory of her charms: the figure in that touching freedom of forgetfulness surprised him; the flush of slumber became her like a flower.

'Upon my word,' he thought, 'I did not think the girl could be so pretty. And to think,' he added, 'that I am under obligation not to use one word of this!' He put forth his stick and touched her; and at that she awoke, sat up with a cry, and looked upon him wildly.

'I trust your Highness has slept well,' he said, nodding.

But she only uttered sounds.

'Compose yourself,' said he, giving her certainly a brave example in his own demeanour. 'My chaise is close at hand; and I shall have, I trust, the singular entertainment of abducting a sovereign Princess.'

'Sir John!' she said, at last.

'At your Highness's disposal,' he replied.

She sprang to her feet. 'O!' she cried, 'have you come from Mittwalden?'

'This morning,' he returned, 'I left it; and if there is any one less likely to return to it than yourself, behold him!'

'The Baron——' she began, and paused.

'Madam,' he answered, 'it was well meant, and you are quite a Judith; but after the hours that have elapsed, you will probably be relieved to hear that he is fairly well. I took his news this morning ere I left. Doing fairly well, they said, but suffering acutely. Hey?—acutely. They could hear his groans in the next room.'

'And the Prince,' she asked, 'is anything known of him?'

'It is reported,' replied Sir John, with the same pleasurable deliberation, 'that upon that point your Highness is the best authority.'

'Sir John,' she said eagerly, 'you were generous enough to speak about your carriage. Will you, I beseech you, will you take me to the Felsenburg? I have business there of an extreme importance.'

'I can refuse you nothing,' replied the old gentleman, gravely and seriously enough. 'Whatever, madam, it is in my power to do for you, that shall be done with pleasure. As soon as my chaise shall overtake us, it is yours to carry you where you will. But,' added he, reverting to his former manner, 'I observe you ask me nothing of the Palace.'

'I do not care,' she said. 'I thought I saw it burning.'

'Prodigious!' said the Baronet. 'You thought? And can the loss of forty toilettes leave you cold? Well, madam, I admire your fortitude. And the state, too? As I left, the government was sitting,—the new government, of which at least two members must be known to you by name: Sabra, who had, I believe, the benefit of being formed in your employment—a footman, am I right?—and our old friend the Chancellor, in something of a subaltern position. But in these convulsions the last shall be first, and the first last.'

'Sir John,' she said, with an air of perfect honesty, 'I am sure you mean most kindly, but these matters have no interest for me.'

The Baronet was so utterly discountenanced that he hailed the appearance of his chaise with welcome, and, by way of saying something, proposed that they should walk back to meet it. So it was done; and he helped her in with courtesy, mounted to her side, and from various receptacles (for the chaise was most completely fitted out) produced fruits and truffled liver, beautiful white bread, and a bottle of delicate wine. With these he served her like a father, coaxing and praising her to fresh exertions; and during all that time, as though silenced by the laws of hospitality, he was not guilty of the shadow of a sneer. Indeed his kindness seemed so genuine that Seraphina was moved to gratitude.

'Sir John,' she said, 'you hate me in your heart; why are you so kind to me?'

'Ah, my good lady,' said he, with no disclaimer of the accusation, 'I have the honour to be much your husband's friend, and somewhat his admirer.'

'You!' she cried. 'They told me you wrote cruelly of both of us.'

'Such was the strange path by which we grew acquainted,' said Sir John. 'I had written, madam, with particular cruelty (since that shall be the phrase) of your fair self. Your husband set me at liberty, gave me a passport, ordered a carriage, and then, with the most boyish spirit, challenged me to fight. Knowing the nature of his married life, I thought the dash and loyalty he showed delightful. "Do not be afraid," says he; "if I am killed, there is nobody to miss me." It appears you subsequently thought of that yourself. But I digress. I explained to him it was impossible that I could fight! "Not if I strike you?" says he. Very droll; I wish I could have put it in my book. However, I was conquered, took the young gentleman to my high favour, and tore up my bits of scandal on the spot. That is one of the little favours, madam, that you owe your husband.'

Seraphina sat for some while in silence. She could bear to be misjudged without a pang by those whom she contemned; she had none of Otto's eagerness to be approved, but went her own way straight and head in air. To Sir John, however, after what he had said, and as her husband's friend, she was prepared to stoop.

'What do you think of me?' she asked abruptly.

'I have told you already,' said Sir John: 'I think you want another glass of my good wine.'

'Come,' she said, 'this is unlike you. You are not wont to be afraid. You say that you admire my husband: in his name, be honest.'

'I admire your courage,' said the Baronet. 'Beyond that, as you have guessed, and indeed said, our natures are not sympathetic.'

'You spoke of scandal,' pursued Seraphina. 'Was the scandal great?'

'It was considerable,' said Sir John.

'And you believed it?' she demanded.

'O, madam,' said Sir John, 'the question!'

'Thank you for that answer!' cried Seraphina. 'And now here, I will tell you, upon my honour, upon my soul, in spite of all the scandal in this world, I am as true a wife as ever stood.'

'We should probably not agree upon a definition,' observed Sir John.

'O!' she cried, 'I have abominably used him—I know that; it is not that I mean. But if you admire my husband, I insist that you shall understand me: I can look him in the face without a blush.'

'It may be, madam,' said Sir John; 'nor have I presumed to think the contrary.'

'You will not believe me?' she cried. 'You think I am a guilty wife? You think he was my lover?'

'Madam,' returned the Baronet, 'when I tore up my papers, I promised your good husband to concern myself no more with your affairs; and I assure you for the last time that I have no desire to judge you.'

'But you will not acquit me! Ah!' she cried, '*he* will—he knows me better!'

Sir John smiled.

'You smile at my distress?' asked Seraphina.

'At your woman's coolness,' said Sir John. 'A man would scarce have had the courage of that cry, which was, for all that, very natural, and I make no doubt quite true. But remark, madam—since you do me the honour to consult me gravely—I have no pity for what you call your distresses. You have been completely selfish, and now reap the consequence. Had you once thought of your husband, instead of singly thinking of yourself, you would not now have been alone, a fugitive, with blood upon your hands, and hearing from a morose old Englishman truth more bitter than scandal.'

'I thank you,' she said, quivering. 'This is very true. Will you stop the carriage?'

'No, child,' said Sir John, 'not until I see you mistress of yourself.'

There was a long pause, during which the carriage rolled by rock and woodland.

'And now,' she resumed, with perfect steadiness, 'will you consider me composed? I request you, as a gentleman, to let me out.'

'I think you do unwisely,' he replied. 'Continue, if you please, to use my carriage.'

'Sir John,' she said, 'if death were sitting on that pile of stones, I would alight! I do not blame, I thank you; I now know how I appear to others; but sooner than draw breath beside a man who can so think of me, I would—O!' she cried, and was silent.

Sir John pulled the string, alighted, and offered her his hand; but she refused the help.

The road had now issued from the valleys in which it had been winding, and come to that part of its course where it runs, like a cornice, along the brow of the steep northward face of Grünewald. The place where they had alighted was at a salient angle; a bold rock and some wind-tortured pine-trees overhung it from above; far below the blue plains lay forth and melted into heaven; and before them the road, by a succession of bold zigzags, was seen mounting to where a tower upon a tall cliff closed the view.

'There,' said the Baronet, pointing to the tower, 'you see the Felsenburg, your goal. I wish you a good journey, and regret I cannot be of more assistance.'

He mounted to his place and gave a signal, and the carriage rolled away.

Seraphina stood by the wayside, gazing before her with blind eyes. Sir John she had dismissed already from her mind: she hated him, that was enough; for whatever Seraphina hated or contemned fell instantly to Lilliputian smallness, and was thenceforward steadily ignored in thought. And now she had matter for concern indeed. Her interview with Otto, which she had never yet forgiven him, began to appear before her in a very different light. He had come to her, still thrilling under recent insult, and not yet breathed from fighting her own cause; and how that knowledge changed the value of his words! Yes, he must have loved her! this was a brave feeling—it was no mere weakness of the will. And she, was she incapable of love? It would appear so; and she swallowed her tears, and yearned to see Otto, to explain all, to ask pity upon her knees for her transgressions, and, if all else were now beyond the reach of reparation, to restore at least the liberty of which she had deprived him.

Swiftly she sped along the highway, and, as the road wound out and in about the bluffs and gullies of the mountain, saw and lost by glimpses the tall tower that stood before and above her, purpled by the mountain air.

CHAPTER II
TREATS OF A CHRISTIAN VIRTUE

When Otto mounted to his rolling prison he found another occupant in a corner of the front seat; but as this person hung his head and the brightness of the carriage lamps shone outward, the Prince could only see it was a man. The Colonel followed his prisoner and clapped-to the door; and at that the four horses broke immediately into a swinging trot.

'Gentlemen,' said the Colonel, after some little while had passed, 'if we are to travel in silence, we might as well be at home. I appear, of course, in an invidious character; but I am a man of taste, fond of books and solidly informing talk, and unfortunately condemned for life to the guard-room. Gentlemen, this is my chance: don't spoil it for me. I have here the pick of the whole court, barring lovely woman; I have a great author in the person of the Doctor—'

'Gotthold!' cried Otto.

'It appears,' said the Doctor bitterly, 'that we must go together. Your Highness had not calculated upon that.'

'What do you infer?' cried Otto; 'that I had you arrested?'

'The inference is simple,' said the Doctor.

'Colonel Gordon,' said the Prince, 'oblige me so far, and set me right with Herr von Hohenstockwitz.'

'Gentlemen,' said the Colonel, 'you are both arrested on the same warrant in the name of the Princess Seraphina, acting regent, countersigned by Prime Minister Freiherr von Gondremark, and dated the day before yesterday, the twelfth. I reveal to you the secrets of the prison-house,' he added.

'Otto,' said Gotthold, 'I ask you to pardon my suspicions.'

'Gotthold,' said the Prince, 'I am not certain I can grant you that.'

'Your Highness is, I am sure, far too magnanimous to hesitate,' said the Colonel. 'But allow me: we speak at home in my religion of the means of grace: and I now propose to offer them.' So saying, the Colonel lighted a bright lamp which he attached to one side of the carriage, and from below the front seat produced a goodly basket adorned with the long necks of bottles. '*Tu spem reducis*—how does it go, Doctor?' he asked gaily. 'I am, in a sense, your host; and I am sure you are both far too considerate of my embarrassing position to refuse to do me honour. Gentlemen, I drink to the Prince!'

'Colonel,' said Otto, 'we have a jovial entertainer. I drink to Colonel Gordon.'

Thereupon all three took their wine very pleasantly; and even as they did so, the carriage with a lurch turned into the high-road and began to make better speed.

All was bright within; the wine had coloured Gotthold's cheek; dim forms of forest trees, dwindling and spiring, scarves of the starry sky, now wide and now narrow, raced past the windows, through one that was left open the air of the woods came in with a nocturnal raciness; and the roll of wheels and the tune of the trotting horses sounded merrily on the ear. Toast followed toast; glass after glass was bowed across and emptied by the trio; and presently there began to fall upon them a luxurious spell, under the influence of which little but the sound of quiet and confidential laughter interrupted the long intervals of meditative silence.

'Otto,' said Gotthold, after one of these seasons of quiet, 'I do not ask you to forgive me. Were the parts reversed, I could not forgive you.'

'Well,' said Otto, 'it is a phrase we use. I do forgive you, but your words and your suspicions rankle; and not yours alone. It is idle, Colonel Gordon, in view of the order you are carrying out, to conceal from you the dissensions of my family; they have gone so far that they are now public property. Well, gentlemen, can I forgive my wife? I can, of course, and do; but in what sense? I would certainly not stoop to any revenge; as certainly I could not think of her but as one changed beyond my recognition.'

'Allow me,' returned the Colonel. 'You will permit me to hope that I am addressing Christians? We are all conscious, I trust, that we are miserable sinners.'

'I disown the consciousness,' said Gotthold. 'Warmed with this good fluid, I deny your thesis.'

'How, sir? You never did anything wrong? and I heard you asking pardon but this moment, not of your God, sir, but of a common fellow-worm!' the Colonel cried.

'I own you have me; you are expert in argument, Herr Oberst,' said the Doctor.

'Begad, sir, I am proud to hear you say so,' said the Colonel. 'I was well grounded indeed at Aberdeen. And as for this matter of forgiveness, it comes, sir, of loose views and (what is if anything more dangerous) a regular life. A sound creed and a bad morality, that's the root of wisdom. You two gentlemen are too good to be forgiving.'

'The paradox is somewhat forced,' said Gotthold.

'Pardon me, Colonel,' said the Prince; 'I readily acquit you of any design of offence, but your words bite like satire. Is this a time, do you think, when I can wish to hear myself called good, now that I am paying the penalty (and am willing like yourself to think it just) of my prolonged misconduct?'

'O, pardon me!' cried the Colonel. 'You have never been expelled from the divinity hall; you have never been broke. I was: broke for a neglect of military duty. To tell you the open truth, your Highness, I was the worse of drink; it's a thing I never do now,' he added, taking out his glass. 'But a man, you see, who has really tasted the defects of his own character, as I have, and has come to regard himself as a kind of blind teetotum knocking about life, begins to learn a very different view about forgiveness. I will talk of not forgiving others, sir, when I have made out to forgive myself, and not before; and the date is like to be a long one. My father, the Reverend Alexander Gordon, was a good man, and damned hard upon others. I am what they call a bad one, and that is just the difference. The man who cannot forgive any mortal thing is a green hand in life.'

'And yet I have heard of you, Colonel, as a duellist,' said Gotthold.

'A different thing, sir,' replied the soldier. 'Professional etiquette. And I trust without unchristian feeling.'

Presently after the Colonel fell into a deep sleep and his companions looked upon each other, smiling.

'An odd fish,' said Gotthold.

'And a strange guardian,' said the Prince. 'Yet what he said was true.'

'Rightly looked upon,' mused Gotthold, 'it is ourselves that we cannot forgive, when we refuse forgiveness to our friend. Some strand of our own misdoing is involved in every quarrel.'

'Are there not offences that disgrace the pardoner?' asked Otto. 'Are there not bounds of self-respect?'

'Otto,' said Gotthold, 'does any man respect himself? To this poor waif of a soldier of fortune we may seem respectable gentlemen; but to ourselves, what are we unless a pasteboard portico and a deliquium of deadly weaknesses within?'

'I? yes,' said Otto; 'but you, Gotthold—you, with your interminable industry, your keen mind, your books—serving mankind, scorning pleasures and temptations! You do not know how I envy you.'

'Otto,' said the Doctor, 'in one word, and a bitter one to say: I am a secret tippler. Yes, I drink too much. The habit has robbed these very books, to which you praise my devotion, of the merits that they should have had. It has spoiled my temper. When I spoke to you the other day, how much of my warmth was in the cause of virtue? how much was the fever of last night's wine? Ay, as my poor fellow-sot there said, and as I vaingloriously denied, we are all miserable sinners, put here for a moment, knowing the good, choosing the evil, standing naked and ashamed in the eye of God.'

'Is it so?' said Otto. 'Why, then, what are we? Are the very best—'

'There is no best in man,' said Gotthold. 'I am not better, it is likely I am not worse, than you or that poor sleeper. I was a sham, and now you know me: that is all.'

'And yet it has not changed my love,' returned Otto softly. 'Our misdeeds do not change us. Gotthold, fill your glass. Let us drink to what is good in this bad business; let us drink to our old affection; and, when we have done so, forgive your too just grounds of offence, and drink with me to my wife, whom I have so misused, who has so misused me, and whom I have left, I fear, I greatly fear, in danger. What matters it how bad we are, if others can still love us, and we can still love others?'

'Ay!' replied the Doctor. 'It is very well said. It is the true answer to the pessimist, and the standing miracle of mankind. So you still love me? and so you can forgive your wife? Why, then, we may bid conscience "Down, dog," like an ill-trained puppy yapping at shadows.'

The pair fell into silence, the Doctor tapping on his empty glass.

The carriage swung forth out of the valleys on that open balcony of high-road that runs along the front of Grünewald, looking down on Gerolstein. Far below, a white waterfall was shining to the stars from the falling skirts of forest, and beyond that, the night stood naked above the plain. On the other hand, the lamp-light skimmed the face of the precipices, and the dwarf pine-trees twinkled with all their needles, and were gone again into the wake. The granite roadway thundered under wheels and hoofs; and at times, by reason of its continual winding, Otto could see the escort on the other side of a ravine, riding well together in the night. Presently the Felsenburg came plainly in view, some way above them, on a bold projection of the mountain, and planting its bulk against the starry sky.

'See, Gotthold,' said the Prince, 'our destination.'

Gotthold awoke as from a trance.

'I was thinking,' said he, 'if there is any danger, why did you not resist? I was told you came of your free will; but should you not be there to help her?'

The colour faded from the Prince's cheeks.

CHAPTER III
PROVIDENCE VON ROSEN: ACT THE LAST
IN WHICH SHE GALLOPS OFF

When the busy Countess came forth from her interview with Seraphina, it is not too much to say that she was beginning to be terribly afraid. She paused in the corridor and reckoned up her doings with an eye to Gondremark. The fan was in requisition in an instant; but her disquiet was beyond the reach of fanning. 'The girl has lost her head,' she thought; and then dismally, 'I have gone too far.' She instantly decided on secession. Now the *Mons Sacer* of the Frau von Rosen was a certain rustic villa in the forest, called by herself, in a smart attack of poesy, Tannen Zauber, and by everybody else plain Kleinbrunn.

Thither, upon the thought, she furiously drove, passing Gondremark at the entrance to the Palace avenue, but feigning not to observe him; and as Kleinbrunn was seven good miles away, and in the bottom of a narrow dell, she passed the night without any rumour of the outbreak reaching her; and the glow of the conflagration was concealed by intervening hills. Frau von Rosen did not sleep well; she was seriously uneasy as to the results of her delightful evening, and saw herself condemned to quite a lengthy sojourn in her deserts and a long defensive correspondence, ere she could venture to return to Gondremark. On the other hand, she examined, by way of pastime, the deeds she had received from Otto; and even here saw cause for disappointment. In these troublous days she had no taste for landed property, and she was convinced, besides, that Otto had paid dearer than the farm was worth. Lastly, the order for the Prince's release fairly burned her meddling fingers.

All things considered, the next day beheld an elegant and beautiful lady, in a riding-habit and a flapping hat, draw bridle at the gate of the Felsenburg, not perhaps with any clear idea of her purpose, but with her usual experimental views on life. Governor Gordon, summoned to the gate, welcomed the omnipotent Countess with his most gallant bearing, though it was wonderful how old he looked in the morning.

'Ah, Governor,' she said, 'we have surprises for you, sir,' and nodded at him meaningly.

'Eh, madam, leave me my prisoners,' he said; 'and if you will but join the band, begad, I'll be happy for life.'

'You would spoil me, would you not?' she asked.

'I would try, I would try,' returned the Governor, and he offered her his arm.

She took it, picked up her skirt, and drew him close to her. 'I have come to see the Prince,' she said. 'Now, infidel! on business. A message from that stupid Gondremark, who keeps me running like a courier. Do I look like one, Herr Gordon?' And she planted her eyes in him.

'You look like an angel, ma'am,' returned the Governor, with a great air of finished gallantry.

The Countess laughed. 'An angel on horseback!' she said. 'Quick work.'

'You came, you saw, you conquered,' flourished Gordon, in high good humour with his own wit and grace. 'We toasted you, madam, in the carriage, in an excellent good glass of wine; toasted you fathom deep; the finest woman, with, begad, the finest eyes in Grünewald. I never saw the like of them but once, in my own country, when I was a young fool at College: Thomasina Haig her name was. I give you my word of honour, she was as like you as two peas.'

'And so you were merry in the carriage?' asked the Countess, gracefully dissembling a yawn.

'We were; we had a very pleasant conversation; but we took perhaps a glass more than that fine fellow of a Prince has been accustomed to,' said the Governor; 'and I observe this morning that he seems a little off his mettle. We'll get him mellow again ere bedtime. This is his door.'

'Well,' she whispered, 'let me get my breath. No, no; wait. Have the door ready to open.' And the Countess, standing like one inspired, shook out her fine voice in 'Lascia ch'io pianga'; and when she had reached the proper point, and lyrically uttered forth her sighings after liberty, the door, at a sign, was flung wide open, and she swam into the Prince's sight, bright-eyed, and with her colour somewhat freshened by the exercise of singing. It was a great dramatic entrance, and to the somewhat doleful prisoner within the sight was sunshine.

'Ah, madam,' he cried, running to her—'you here!'

She looked meaningly at Gordon; and as soon as the door was closed she fell on Otto's neck. 'To see you here!' she moaned and clung to him.

But the Prince stood somewhat stiffly in that enviable situation, and the Countess instantly recovered from her outburst.

'Poor child,' she said, 'poor child! Sit down beside me here, and tell me all about it. My heart really bleeds to see you. How does time go?'

'Madam,' replied the Prince, sitting down beside her, his gallantry recovered, 'the time will now go all too quickly till you leave. But I must ask you for the news. I have most bitterly condemned myself for my inertia of last night. You wisely counselled me; it was my duty to resist. You wisely and nobly counselled me; I have since thought of it with wonder. You have a noble heart.'

'Otto,' she said, 'spare me. Was it even right, I wonder? I have duties, too, you poor child; and when I see you they all melt—all my good resolutions fly away.'

'And mine still come too late,' he replied, sighing. 'O, what would I not give to have resisted? What would I not give for freedom?'

'Well, what would you give?' she asked; and the red fan was spread; only her eyes, as if from over battlements, brightly surveyed him.

'I? What do you mean? Madam, you have some news for me,' he cried.

'O, O!' said madam dubiously.

He was at her feet. 'Do not trifle with my hopes,' he pleaded. 'Tell me, dearest Madame von Rosen, tell me! You cannot be cruel: it is not in your nature. Give? I can give nothing; I have nothing; I can only plead in mercy.'

'Do not,' she said; 'it is not fair. Otto, you know my weakness. Spare me. Be generous.'

'O, madam,' he said, 'it is for you to be generous, to have pity.' He took her hand and pressed it; he plied her with caresses and appeals. The Countess had a most enjoyable sham siege, and then relented. She sprang to her feet, she tore her dress open, and, all warm from her bosom, threw the order on the floor.

'There!' she cried. 'I forced it from her. Use it, and I am ruined!' And she turned away as if to veil the force of her emotions.

Otto sprang upon the paper, read it, and cried out aloud. 'O, God bless her!' he said, 'God bless her.' And he kissed the writing.

Von Rosen was a singularly good-natured woman, but her part was now beyond her. 'Ingrate!' she cried; 'I wrung it from her, I betrayed my trust to get it, and 'tis she you thank!'

'Can you blame me?' said the Prince. 'I love her.'

'I see that,' she said. 'And I?'

'You, Madame von Rosen? You are my dearest, my kindest, and most generous of friends,' he said, approaching her. 'You would be a perfect friend, if you were not so lovely. You have a great sense of humour, you cannot be unconscious of your charm, and you amuse yourself at times by playing on my weakness; and at times I can take pleasure in the comedy. But not to-day: to-day you will be the true, the serious, the manly friend, and you will suffer me to forget that you are lovely and that I am weak. Come, dear Countess, let me to-day repose in you entirely.'

He held out his hand, smiling, and she took it frankly. 'I vow you have bewitched me,' she said; and then with a laugh, 'I break my staff!' she added; 'and I must pay you my best compliment. You made a difficult speech. You are as adroit, dear Prince, as I am—charming.' And as she said the word with a great curtsey, she justified it.

'You hardly keep the bargain, madam, when you make yourself so beautiful,' said the Prince, bowing.

'It was my last arrow,' she returned. 'I am disarmed. Blank cartridge, *O mon Prince*! And now I tell you, if you choose to leave this prison, you can, and I am ruined. Choose!'

'Madame von Rosen,' replied Otto, 'I choose, and I will go. My duty points me, duty still neglected by this Featherhead. But do not fear to be a loser. I propose instead that you should take me with you, a bear in chains, to Baron Gondremark. I am become perfectly unscrupulous: to save my wife I will do all, all he can ask or fancy. He shall be filled; were he huge as leviathan and greedy as the grave, I will content him. And you, the fairy of our pantomime, shall have the credit.'

'Done!' she cried. 'Admirable! Prince Charming no longer—Prince Sorcerer, Prince Solon! Let us go this moment. Stay,' she cried, pausing. 'I beg dear Prince, to give you back these deeds. 'Twas you who liked the farm—I have not seen it; and it was you who wished to benefit the peasants. And, besides,' she added, with a comical change of tone, 'I should prefer the ready money.'

Both laughed. 'Here I am, once more a farmer,' said Otto, accepting the papers, 'but overwhelmed in debt.'

The Countess touched a bell, and the Governor appeared.

'Governor,' she said, 'I am going to elope with his Highness. The result of our talk has been a thorough understanding, and the *coup d'état* is over. Here is the order.'

Colonel Gordon adjusted silver spectacles upon his nose. 'Yes,' he said, 'the Princess: very right. But the warrant, madam, was countersigned.'

'By Heinrich!' said von Rosen. 'Well, and here am I to represent him.'

'Well, your Highness,' resumed the soldier of fortune, 'I must congratulate you upon my loss. You have been cut out by beauty, and I am left lamenting. The Doctor still remains to me: *probus, doctus, lepidus, jucundus*: a man of books.'

'Ay, there is nothing about poor Gotthold,' said the Prince.

'The Governor's consolation? Would you leave him bare?' asked von Rosen.

'And, your Highness,' resumed Gordon, 'may I trust that in the course of this temporary obscuration, you have found me discharge my part with suitable respect and, I may add, tact? I adopted purposely a cheerfulness of manner; mirth, it appeared to me, and a good glass of wine, were the fit alleviations.'

'Colonel,' said Otto, holding out his hand, 'your society was of itself enough. I do not merely thank you for your pleasant spirits; I have to thank you, besides, for some philosophy, of which I stood in need. I trust I do not see you for the last time; and in the meanwhile, as a memento of our strange acquaintance, let me offer you these verses on which I was but now engaged. I am so little of a poet, and was so ill inspired by prison bars, that they have some claim to be at least a curiosity.'

The Colonel's countenance lighted as he took the paper; the silver spectacles were hurriedly replaced. 'Ha!' he said, 'Alexandrines, the tragic metre. I shall cherish this, your Highness, like a relic; no more suitable offering, although I say it, could be made. "*Dieux de l'immense plaine et des vastes forêts*." Very good,' he said, 'very good indeed! "*Et du geôlier lui-même apprendre des leçons*." Most handsome, begad!'

'Come, Governor,' cried the Countess, 'you can read his poetry when we are gone. Open your grudging portals.'

'I ask your pardon,' said the Colonel. 'To a man of my character and tastes, these verses, this handsome reference—most moving, I assure you. Can I offer you an escort?'

'No, no,' replied the Countess. 'We go incogniti, as we arrived. We ride together; the Prince will take my servant's horse. Hurry and privacy, Herr Oberst, that is all we seek.' And she began impatiently to lead the way.

But Otto had still to bid farewell to Dr. Gotthold; and the Governor following, with his spectacles in one hand and the paper in the other, had still to communicate his treasured verses, piece by piece, as he succeeded in deciphering the manuscript, to all he came across; and still his enthusiasm mounted. 'I declare,' he cried at last, with the air of one who has at length divined a mystery, 'they remind me of Robbie Burns!'

But there is an end to all things; and at length Otto was walking by the side of Madame von Rosen, along that mountain wall, her servant following with both the horses, and all about them sunlight, and breeze, and flying bird, and the vast regions of the air, and the capacious prospect: wildwood and climbing pinnacle, and the sound and voice of mountain torrents, at their hand: and far below them, green melting into sapphire on the plains.

They walked at first in silence; for Otto's mind was full of the delight of liberty and nature, and still, betweenwhiles, he was preparing his interview with Gondremark. But when the first rough promontory of the rock was turned, and the Felsenburg concealed behind its bulk, the lady paused.

'Here,' she said, 'I will dismount poor Karl, and you and I must ply our spurs. I love a wild ride with a good companion.'

As she spoke, a carriage came into sight round the corner next below them in the order of the road. It came heavily creaking, and a little ahead of it a traveller was soberly walking, note-book in hand.

'It is Sir John,' cried Otto, and he hailed him.

The Baronet pocketed his note-book, stared through an eye-glass, and then waved his stick; and he on his side, and the Countess and the Prince on theirs, advanced with somewhat quicker steps. They met at the re-entrant angle, where a thin stream sprayed across a boulder and was scattered in rain among the brush; and the Baronet saluted the Prince with much punctilio. To the Countess, on the other hand, he bowed with a kind of sneering wonder.

'Is it possible, madam, that you have not heard the news?' he asked.

'What news?' she cried.

'News of the first order,' returned Sir John: 'a revolution in the State, a Republic declared, the palace burned to the ground, the Princess in flight, Gondremark wounded—'

'Heinrich wounded?' she screamed.

'Wounded and suffering acutely,' said Sir John. 'His groans—'

There fell from the lady's lips an oath so potent that, in smoother hours, it would have made her hearers jump. She ran to her horse, scrambled to the saddle, and, yet half seated, dashed down the road at full gallop. The groom, after a pause of wonder, followed her. The rush of her impetuous passage almost scared the carriage horses over the verge of the steep hill;

and still she clattered further, and the crags echoed to her flight, and still the groom flogged vainly in pursuit of her. At the fourth corner, a woman trailing slowly up leaped back with a cry and escaped death by a hand's-breadth. But the Countess wasted neither glance nor thought upon the incident. Out and in, about the bluffs of the mountain wall, she fled, loose-reined, and still the groom toiled in her pursuit.

'A most impulsive lady!' said Sir John. 'Who would have thought she cared for him?' And before the words were uttered, he was struggling in the Prince's grasp.

'My wife! the Princess? What of her?'

'She is down the road,' he gasped. 'I left her twenty minutes back.'

And next moment, the choked author stood alone, and the Prince on foot was racing down the hill behind the Countess.

CHAPTER IV
BABES IN THE WOOD

While the feet of the Prince continued to run swiftly, his heart, which had at first by far outstripped his running, soon began to linger and hang back. Not that he ceased to pity the misfortune or to yearn for the sight of Seraphina; but the memory of her obdurate coldness awoke within him, and woke in turn his own habitual diffidence of self. Had Sir John been given time to tell him all, had he even known that she was speeding to the Felsenburg, he would have gone to her with ardour. As it was, he began to see himself once more intruding, profiting, perhaps, by her misfortune, and now that she was fallen, proffering unloved caresses to the wife who had spurned him in prosperity. The sore spots upon his vanity began to burn; once more, his anger assumed the carriage of a hostile generosity; he would utterly forgive indeed; he would help, save, and comfort his unloving wife; but all with distant self-denial, imposing silence on his heart, respecting Seraphina's disaffection as he would the innocence of a child. So, when at length he turned a corner and beheld the Princess, it was his first thought to reassure her of the purity of his respect, and he at once ceased running and stood still. She, upon her part, began to run to him with a little cry; then, seeing him pause, she paused also, smitten with remorse; and at length, with the most guilty timidity, walked nearly up to where he stood.

'Otto,' she said, 'I have ruined all!'

'Seraphina!' he cried with a sob, but did not move, partly withheld by his resolutions, partly struck stupid at the sight of her weariness and disorder. Had she stood silent, they had soon been locked in an embrace. But she too had prepared herself against the interview, and must spoil the golden hour with protestations.

'All!' she went on, 'I have ruined all! But, Otto, in kindness you must hear me—not justify, but own, my faults. I have been taught so cruelly; I have had such time for thought, and see the world so changed. I have been blind, stone-blind; I have let all true good go by me, and lived on shadows. But when this dream fell, and I had betrayed you, and thought I had killed—' She paused. 'I thought I had killed Gondremark,' she said with a deep flush, 'and I found myself alone, as you said.'

The mention of the name of Gondremark pricked the Princes generosity like a spur. 'Well,' he cried, 'and whose fault was it but mine? It was my duty to be beside you, loved or not. But I was a skulker in the grain, and found it easier to desert than to oppose you. I could never learn that better part of love, to fight love's battles. But yet the love was there. And now when this toy kingdom of ours has fallen, first of all by my demerits, and next by your inexperience, and we are here alone together, as poor as Job and merely a man and a woman—let me conjure you to forgive the weakness and to repose in the love. Do not mistake me!' he cried, seeing her about to speak, and imposing silence with uplifted hand. 'My love is changed; it is purged of any conjugal pretension; it does not ask, does not hope, does not wish for a return in kind. You may forget for ever that part in which you found me so distasteful, and accept without embarrassment the affection of a brother.'

'You are too generous, Otto,' she said. 'I know that I have forfeited your love. I cannot take this sacrifice. You had far better leave me. O, go away, and leave me to my fate!'

'O no!' said Otto; 'we must first of all escape out of this hornet's nest, to which I led you. My honour is engaged. I said but now we were as poor as Job; and behold! not many miles from here I have a house of my own to which I will conduct you. Otto the Prince being down, we must try what luck remains to Otto the Hunter. Come, Seraphina; show that you forgive me, and let us set about this business of escape in the best spirits possible. You used to say, my dear, that, except as a husband and a prince, I was a pleasant fellow. I am neither now, and you may like my company without remorse. Come, then; it were idle to be captured. Can you still walk? Forth, then,' said he, and he began to lead the way.

A little below where they stood, a good-sized brook passed below the road, which overleapt it in a single arch. On one bank of that loquacious water a foot-path descended a green dell. Here it was rocky and stony, and lay on the steep scarps of the ravine; here it was choked with brambles; and there, in fairy haughs, it lay for a few paces evenly on the green turf. Like a sponge, the hillside oozed with well-water. The burn kept growing both in force and volume; at every leap it fell with heavier plunges and span more widely in the pool. Great had been the labours of that stream, and great and agreeable the changes it had wrought. It had cut through dykes of stubborn rock, and now, like a blowing dolphin, spouted through the orifice; along all its humble coasts, it had undermined and rafted-down the goodlier timber of the forest; and on these rough clearings it now set and tended primrose gardens, and planted woods of willow, and made a favourite of the silver birch. Through all these friendly features the path, its human acolyte, conducted our two wanderers downward,—Otto before, still pausing at the more difficult passages to lend assistance; the Princess following. From time to time, when he turned to help her, her face would lighten upon his—her eyes, half desperately, woo him. He saw, but dared not understand. 'She does not love me,' he told himself, with magnanimity. 'This is remorse or gratitude; I were no gentleman, no, nor yet a man, if I presumed upon these pitiful concessions.'

Some way down the glen, the stream, already grown to a good bulk of water, was rudely dammed across, and about a third of it abducted in a wooden trough. Gaily the pure water, air's first cousin, fleeted along the rude aqueduct, whose sides and floor it had made green with grasses. The path, bearing it close company, threaded a wilderness of briar and wild-rose. And presently, a little in front, the brown top of a mill and the tall mill-wheel, spraying diamonds, arose in the narrows of the glen; at the same time the snoring music of the saws broke the silence.

The miller, hearing steps, came forth to his door, and both he and Otto started.

'Good-morning, miller,' said the Prince. 'You were right, it seems, and I was wrong. I give you the news, and bid you to Mittwalden. My throne has fallen—great was the fall of it!—and your good friends of the Phoenix bear the rule.'

The red-faced miller looked supreme astonishment. 'And your Highness?' he gasped.

'My Highness is running away,' replied Otto, 'straight for the frontier.'

'Leaving Grünewald?' cried the man. 'Your father's son? It's not to be permitted!'

'Do you arrest us, friend?' asked Otto, smiling.

'Arrest you? I?' exclaimed the man. 'For what does your Highness take me? Why, sir, I make sure there is not a man in Grünewald would lay hands upon you.'

'O, many, many,' said the Prince; 'but from you, who were bold with me in my greatness, I should even look for aid in my distress.'

The miller became the colour of beetroot. 'You may say so indeed,' said he. 'And meanwhile, will you and your lady step into my house.'

'We have not time for that,' replied the Prince; 'but if you would oblige us with a cup of wine without here, you will give a pleasure and a service, both in one.'

The miller once more coloured to the nape. He hastened to bring forth wine in a pitcher and three bright crystal tumblers. 'Your Highness must not suppose,' he said, as he filled them, 'that I am an habitual drinker. The time when I had the misfortune to encounter you, I was a trifle overtaken, I allow; but a more sober man than I am in my ordinary, I do not know where you are to look for; and even this glass that I drink to you (and to the lady) is quite an unusual recreation.'

The wine was drunk with due rustic courtesies; and then, refusing further hospitality, Otto and Seraphina once more proceeded to descend the glen, which now began to open and to be invaded by the taller trees.

'I owed that man a reparation,' said the Prince; 'for when we met I was in the wrong and put a sore affront upon him. I judge by myself, perhaps; but I begin to think that no one is the better for a humiliation.'

'But some have to be taught so,' she replied.

'Well, well,' he said, with a painful embarrassment. 'Well, well. But let us think of safety. My miller is all very good, but I do not pin my faith to him. To follow down this stream will bring us, but after innumerable windings, to my house. Here, up this glade, there lies a cross-cut—the world's end for solitude—the very deer scarce visit it. Are you too tired, or could you pass that way?'

'Choose the path, Otto. I will follow you,' she said.

'No,' he replied, with a singular imbecility of manner and appearance, 'but I meant the path was rough. It lies, all the way, by glade and dingle, and the dingles are both deep and thorny.'

'Lead on,' she said. 'Are you not Otto the Hunter?'

They had now burst across a veil of underwood, and were come into a lawn among the forest, very green and innocent, and solemnly surrounded by trees. Otto paused on the margin, looking about him with delight; then his glance returned to Seraphina, as she stood framed in that silvan pleasantness and looking at her husband with undecipherable eyes. A weakness both of the body and mind fell on him like the beginnings of sleep; the cords of his activity were relaxed, his eyes clung to her. 'Let us rest,' he said; and he made her sit down, and himself sat down beside her on the slope of an inconsiderable mound.

She sat with her eyes downcast, her slim hand dabbling in grass, like a maid waiting for love's summons. The sound of the wind in the forest swelled and sank, and drew near them with a running rush, and died away and away in the distance into fainting whispers. Nearer hand, a bird out of the deep covert uttered broken and anxious notes. All this seemed but a halting prelude to speech. To Otto it seemed as if the whole frame of nature were waiting for his words; and yet his pride kept him silent. The longer he watched that slender and pale hand plucking at the grasses, the harder and rougher grew the fight between pride and its kindly adversary.

'Seraphina,' he said at last, 'it is right you should know one thing: I never . .
.' He was about to say 'doubted you,' but was that true? And, if true, was it
generous to speak of it? Silence succeeded.

'I pray you, tell it me,' she said; 'tell it me, in pity.'

'I mean only this,' he resumed, 'that I understand all, and do not blame
you. I understand how the brave woman must look down on the weak
man. I think you were wrong in some things; but I have tried to
understand it, and I do. I do not need to forget or to forgive, Seraphina,
for I have understood.'

'I know what I have done,' she said. 'I am not so weak that I can be
deceived with kind speeches. I know what I have been—I see myself. I
am not worth your anger, how much less to be forgiven! In all this
downfall and misery, I see only me and you: you, as you have been always;
me, as I was—me, above all! O yes, I see myself: and what can I think?'

'Ah, then, let us reverse the parts!' said Otto. 'It is ourselves we cannot
forgive, when we deny forgiveness to another—so a friend told me last
night. On these terms, Seraphina, you see how generously *I* have forgiven
myself. But am not I to be forgiven? Come, then, forgive yourself—and
me.'

She did not answer in words, but reached out her hand to him quickly. He
took it; and as the smooth fingers settled and nestled in his, love ran to and
fro between them in tender and transforming currents.

'Seraphina,' he cried, 'O, forget the past! Let me serve and help you; let me
be your servant; it is enough for me to serve you and to be near you; let me
be near you, dear—do not send me away.' He hurried his pleading like the
speech of a frightened child. 'It is not love,' he went on; 'I do not ask for
love; my love is enough . . .'

'Otto!' she said, as if in pain.

He looked up into her face. It was wrung with the very ecstasy of
tenderness and anguish; on her features, and most of all in her changed
eyes, there shone the very light of love.

'Seraphina?' he cried aloud, and with a sudden, tuneless voice, 'Seraphina?'

'Look round you at this glade,' she cried, 'and where the leaves are coming
on young trees, and the flowers begin to blossom. This is where we meet,
meet for the first time; it is so much better to forget and to be born again.
O what a pit there is for sins—God's mercy, man's oblivion!'

'Seraphina,' he said, 'let it be so, indeed; let all that was be merely the abuse
of dreaming; let me begin again, a stranger. I have dreamed, in a long

dream, that I adored a girl unkind and beautiful; in all things my superior, but still cold, like ice. And again I dreamed, and thought she changed and melted, glowed and turned to me. And I—who had no merit but a love, slavish and unerect—lay close, and durst not move for fear of waking.'

'Lie close,' she said, with a deep thrill of speech.

So they spake in the spring woods; and meanwhile, in Mittwalden Rath-haus, the Republic was declared.

BIBLIOGRAPHICAL POSTSCRIPT TO COMPLETE THE STORY

The reader well informed in modern history will not require details as to the fate of the Republic. The best account is to be found in the memoirs of Herr Greisengesang (7 Bände: Leipzig), by our passing acquaintance the licentiate Roederer. Herr Roederer, with too much of an author's licence, makes a great figure of his hero—poses him, indeed, to be the centre-piece and cloud-compeller of the whole. But, with due allowance for this bias, the book is able and complete.

The reader is of course acquainted with the vigorous and bracing pages of Sir John (2 vols., London: Longman, Hurst, Rees, Orme and Brown). Sir John, who plays but a tooth-comb in the orchestra of this historical romance, blows in his own book the big bassoon. His character is there drawn at large; and the sympathy of Landor has countersigned the admiration of the public. One point, however, calls for explanation; the chapter on Grünewald was torn by the hand of the author in the palace gardens; how comes it, then, to figure at full length among my more modest pages, the Lion of the caravan? That eminent literatus was a man of method; 'Juvenal by double entry,' he was once profanely called; and when he tore the sheets in question, it was rather, as he has since explained, in the search for some dramatic evidence of his sincerity, than with the thought of practical deletion. At that time, indeed, he was possessed of two blotted scrolls and a fair copy in double. But the chapter, as the reader knows, was honestly omitted from the famous 'Memoirs on the various Courts of Europe.' It has been mine to give it to the public.

Bibliography still helps us with a further glimpse of our characters. I have here before me a small volume (printed for private circulation: no printer's name; n.d.), 'Poésies par Frédéric et Amélie.' Mine is a presentation copy, obtained for me by Mr. Bain in the Haymarket; and the name of the first owner is written on the fly-leaf in the hand of Prince Otto himself. The modest epigraph—'Le rime n'est pas riche'—may be attributed, with a good show of likelihood, to the same collaborator. It is strikingly appropriate, and I have found the volume very dreary. Those pieces in which I seem to trace the hand of the Princess are particularly dull and conscientious. But the booklet had a fair success with that public for which it was designed; and I have come across some evidences of a second venture of the same sort, now unprocurable. Here, at least, we may take leave of Otto and Seraphina—what do I say? of Frédéric and Amélie—

ageing together peaceably at the court of the wife's father, jingling French rhymes and correcting joint proofs.

Still following the book-lists, I perceive that Mr. Swinburne has dedicated a rousing lyric and some vigorous sonnets to the memory of Gondremark; that name appears twice at least in Victor Hugo's trumpet-blasts of patriot enumeration; and I came latterly, when I supposed my task already ended, on a trace of the fallen politician and his Countess. It is in the 'Diary of J. Hogg Cotterill, Esq.' (that very interesting work). Mr. Cotterill, being at Naples, is introduced (May 27th) to 'a Baron and Baroness Gondremark— he a man who once made a noise—she still beautiful—both witty. She complimented me much upon my French—should never have known me to be English—had known my uncle, Sir John, in Germany—recognised in me, as a family trait, some of his *grand air* and studious courtesy—asked me to call.' And again (May 30th), 'visited the Baronne de Gondremark— much gratified—a most *refined, intelligent* woman, quite of the old school, now, *hélas*! extinct—had read my *Remarks on Sicily*—it reminds her of my uncle, but with more of grace—I feared she thought there was less energy—assured no—a softer style of presentation, more of the *literary grace*, but the same firm grasp of circumstance and force of thought—in short, just Buttonhole's opinion. Much encouraged. I have a real esteem for this patrician lady.' The acquaintance lasted some time; and when Mr. Cotterill left in the suite of Lord Protocol, and, as he is careful to inform us, in Admiral Yardarm's flag-ship, one of his chief causes of regret is to leave 'that most *spirituelle* and sympathetic lady, who already regards me as a younger brother.'

Milton Keynes UK
Ingram Content Group UK Ltd.
UKHW030624061024
449204UK00004B/328

9 789362 097385